MAKING GAME

Peter and Linn at age 19

MAKING GAME

An Essay on Hunting, Familiar Things,
and the Strangeness of Being Who One Is

PETER L. ATKINSON

AU PRESS

© 2009 Peter L. Atkinson

Published by AU Press, Athabasca University
1200, 10011 – 109 Street
Edmonton, AB T5J 3S8

Atkinson, Peter, 1952–
    Making game: an essay on hunting, familiar things,
and the strangeness of being who one is / Peter Atkinson.

(Cultural dialectics 1915-836x)
Also available in electronic format.
ISBN 978-1-897425-28-2

1. Atkinson, Peter, 1952–. 2. Hunting – Philosophy. 3. Hunting –
Moral and ethical aspects. 5. Hunters – United States–Biography.
I. Title. II. Series: Cultural dialectics series (Print)

SK17.A85A3 2008   799.292   C2008-907672-9

Printed and bound in Canada by AGMV Marquis

Layout and book design by Infoscan Collette, Quebec City
Cover design by Nancy Biamonte
Frontispiece photo by Stephen Bulloch

Please contact AU Press, Athabasca University at
aupress@athabascau.ca for permission beyond the usage
outlined in the Creative Commons license.

For Linn and our boys.

Contents

Acknowledgments ix

Zero 1

One 5

Two 21

Three 57

Four 71

Five 85

Six 97

Seven 107

Eight 123

Nine 141

Acknowledgments

I should like to acknowledge just a handful of the persons still living without whom, no matter how poorly made, these pages could not have been written: my brothers, Matthew and Leeds; Stuart Hutson, for quail and a long friendship in the wild; Thomas Brown for elk, Harvey Mudd for fly fishing and my first taste of the west; J. Mark Smith for his intellectual companionship; Glen Davis for teaching me how to read; Robert T. Cooke, for years of encouragement; John Sanders for his example; and, beyond all others, James McMichael.

Zero

0.0

Even if more frightened than hurt, a dog that has been injured will sometimes hide until his desire for a meal and his place near the fire grows stronger than his fear. When we were eighteen, my childhood sweetheart and I ran away together. Or we clung to one another as our families dissolved around us. In either case, I experienced her as if a window in a very hot room had been thrown open and when I looked about I was no longer a child. Within seven years, she was wife to me and mother to our eldest son – another was to come. We were together for almost fifteen years and now have lived apart longer than that. The marriage is something that exists in fits and starts along certain lines of narrative. Some of these tracks are habitual. Others have grown vague or perhaps even vanished. Our time together has become a dream we dream more or less separately. However, I find I have been party to raising two boys. They visit. Know me as father. As with a great deal that has been crucial, having children was not my idea. The point is that after being together for six years, and while we were both still in college, my girlfriend, who had shown almost no inclination towards children, announced one afternoon that she wanted a baby. I wanted to hide.

One

1.0

Before a light breeze and on the flooding tide, a heavy wooden schooner slipped into Long Island Sound with remarkable speed. Pushed up by a flat stem, the bow wave crumbled into the confused water rolling down the boot topping. We were fishing for late season stripers off Orient Point and had anchored the open launch mid-channel in the morning fog. The engine was off. Led out through the port chock, our anchor-rode went slack and taut by turns as the skiff bounced in the steep chop kicked up by the tide. Horsing against a four knot current on shortened scope, our light ground tackle had to have been dragging across the uneven bottom.

In the Gut, the channel formed between Plum Island and Orient Point, the stripers can be huge. The local paper has reported them as large as eighty pounds, and every year one over fifty pounds gets taken. These big bass tuck themselves into the rocks and wait. Protected from the force of the tide, they feed on what gets swept by. Trout are also prone to lie just outside the fast water, behind a rock or at the end of a riffle and wait for the current to bring them insects and little fish.

The schooner's eighty tons glided by us so quietly that if I had been looking the other way I might have missed her. Surely we had been taking a risk anchored as we were in the fog. But from the moment she first ghosted into view, it was clear she was going to pass close down our starboard side. I was never afraid. As if in slow motion, I found myself to be in the midst of all that was happening. Her showing up unfolded with and like the folding of the bow wave at her stem. I am not sure if it is possible to be struck by the uncanny and be afraid at the same time.

The sense of the strange that rolled over me with the schooner's appearance did not interrupt what I was doing. I kept fishing. As I held to my pole, my attention remained attached to the tension in my line let out on the stern. All activity continued without pause even if not quite as before. For things felt different than they had. Caught up in a conspicuous sense of being there, I had run up on a set of circumstances that had somehow been there all along. The situation was in this sense familiar. I had been there all along fishing from the skiff but in a certain modality of not being there. If I am daydreaming and thinking of other things, this is yet another way I may not be there. But I had been not been lost in thought or far away. I had been lost in fishing. As the schooner materialized in the fog, what began to loom was a sense of mystery concerning a darkness that usually keeps from sense both the whence of coming and the whither of going. This strange and yet familiar shadow is usually washed out in the light of the obvious.

1.1

Last year, north of Wilcox, Arizona, on a hillside flanking the long wash running down to one of Stuart's favorite tanks a singular Gambel's cock broke cover and fixed in the deepest part of memory. I had already killed him: a shattered wing, the other beating in disordered pulses, his eyes faintly giving back the desert sky, the winter image of clouds and of clouding. A magnificent bird, he was the largest I had seen that year: a "real chicken."

It was unseasonably warm, too warm for the young dogs to gather much scent. I had bumped up the bird myself. After I shot the cock and took him from Nora's mouth, I looked at him a little longer than is probably usual, reached blindly and settled him down with the other quail in the game bag hanging from the back of my vest. But when that bird had broken cover and I had pulled the barrels of my double-gun along the path of his flight, just before I pulled the trigger, I was there in the midst of swinging my gun to the track of the bird. The sense of catching myself at hunting this bird was not quite the same as catching sight of myself; it was not as if I suddenly saw myself from afar. I had not been watching myself hunt. I had just happened upon myself. Intent on killing that bird and for no obvious reason, I had emerged from a kind of wholeness: the landscape and bird all bound up together in the act of hunting. The bird was the center of this feeling: a bird, not so much different from any other bird I had killed that afternoon. This encounter with myself was thick enough to hold the hunting of the cock in place. My awareness never broke. I squeezed the trigger, watched the cock fold up, hit the ground, flutter and die – all within a pervading sense of what was familiar and what was strange. Drenched in the real.

1.2

When I was ten years old we lived in a shingled house on top of a steep hill that overlooked Flax Pond. Beyond the tidal marsh, Long Island stretched away from what was at that time the end of suburbia and the beginning of exurbia. Eighty years before the whole neck had been a horse farm belonging to one of the robber barons. The estate lost its way sometime between the wars and was broken up into separate holdings. A couple of huge beech trees were all that remained of the landscaping around the main house then lost to the encroaching woods: shade trees on what was once a vast sloping lawn. The industrialist's house was a big affair with a long sweeping stair situated a couple of hundred yards or so from a collection of horse barns and a series of corrals. All these buildings were slowly falling apart, full of pigeons and feral cats. We lived in what had been the caretaker's house a couple of hundred yards away on a hill above the barns. In the early sixties, just as this part of the world was starting to get expensive again, there was still a lot of open space in which children could play.

Some of the neighboring kids were there. We were involved in a military game that included a lot of running around the house. I was in the process of ambushing a group of my playmates with a wooden machine gun, which I had made in the basement fro m scraps of wood, bits of hose and the like. Quite in the middle of everything, or perhaps equivalently, out of nowhere, I was met by the odd experience of being who I was. I abruptly encountered myself as I was; a feeling of contingency anchored to a sense of having to be was upon me. I had shown up from nowhere as the one who was involved in what was going on and, just as I became interested in this strange feeling and without transition, I continued to machine-gun my little friends running madly on the lawn. Feelings lapsed into memory. The uncanny sense of myself being vanished the moment I reached for it. The whole of things was everywhere, and then nowhere at all. A twinge of disappointment flashed as the explicitness of myself waned back into the excitement of our game, and I was left with a subtle sense that I had encountered a truth that had evaporated before I ever quite saw it. The fragility of the uncanny is palpable. Yet after close to forty years, I continue to call upon an impression of how I had felt on that hillside as a child: both when I emerged from my game and when the feeling disappeared.

1.3

If there are seams or transitions between my moods and feelings, I never experience them. When or if I check myself, I already have a mood, am already disposed towards the world in this way or that. Mood is not an intrusion into how things are. It is synonymous with how things are. My dog chewed up my shoe. I was momentarily surprised and then, without transition, I was in a state. Dismay flashed into anger. My mind wandered. When I returned from following down the stream of thought and feeling, I was only mildly irritated. I formed an image of the dog chewing my shoe. I had been angry but when I looked again the whole episode, myself included, seemed ridiculous or even amusing. When I investigate, I always find myself to be precisely as I am: surprised, dismayed, angry, irritated or amused. I never find myself to be partially as I am, or on my way towards being as I am. That 'I am precisely as I am' is what I have in mind when I speak of the wholeness of my mood, or simply the wholeness of my way to be. The wholeness of who I am is not merely an idea. It is something felt.

The phenomenon of wholeness is experienced when I emerge from a complete or perfect absorption in activity. 'I' becomes who it is in its emergence from the undifferentiated wholeness of happening. Wholeness is a phenomenon that is never faithfully reproduced or fully ascertained in a proposition. Every attempt to articulate the sense of unity that is felt in the emergence of self from its utter engagement with the world must run the risk of becoming a positing and as such changing the kind of being that belongs to the unity of what is whole.

A whole may have parts, but wholeness or unity does not. To articulate something means to move it at its joints and so in this way to make present how it is going. This 'it' is something like the it that snows in winter when it is cold or rains in the spring when it is raining. Because wholeness has no components – no knuckles – it is moot to speak of bending wholeness at its joints. Every expression of wholeness is a feat of imagination that grows from a projection of, or an idea concerning, the unity that constitutes the phenomenon. Every view of wholeness has already posited something outside that wholeness from which the phenomenon is seen. But since wholeness includes everything, there is no place or vantage belonging to wholeness from which the rest of it can be seen. When I imagine wholeness, I imagine it as something over there and away from me. And so in gaining a view of wholeness, that wholeness fails to encompass the position from which it has been imagined. As something imagined, wholeness fails to comprehend the one who is trying to comprehend it. Wholeness becomes contextualized in the very act of being posited. But the whole is precisely that which exceeds or exhausts every context. Wholeness has no context. So in every articulation of the whole of things, the very being of this wholeness is in danger of being taken up as otherwise.

By way of analogy, nothingness has a relation to expression that is similar to the relation wholeness has. Just as wholeness cannot be articulated without opening up the possibility that what has been posited will contextualizing itself and so depriving itself of its most essential character (something like a lack of boundary), nothing cannot be posited without changing what it is supposed to mean. To utter the word 'nothing' points nothing out in the sense of making nothing present. And so in the act of being pointed out, of being posited, nothing becomes all too much like something. This is not a problem but a fact.

The mood of the familiar-strange is the uncanny sense of the obvious. In the unexpected emergence of myself from the wholeness of engaged activity within my environment, I encounter myself. *I am* and *the world is* familiar in an obvious way. But it is this obviousness that is strange. How is it that I am struck by the fact of myself? Who else was I expecting? In being caught within the mood of the familiar-strange, I do not run into an alteration between something that is familiar and then something else that is strange. Familiarity and strangeness, which permeates the explicit sense of my being caught up in contingency in a way that cannot be otherwise, are manifestly inseparable. Neither do I mean that the distinction between the familiar and the strange either fails to constitute a real distinction or that the distinction is not useful. I only mean that there is a difference between the experience of the familiar-strange and the positing of that same experience as familiar and then strange. In the familiar-strange encounter with myself in which I am taken over by a dynamic sense of an impossible wholeness, I feel as if all of what I am has been given over to the incalculable and logically diffident unity of that which is contingent and that which is necessary.

The dynamic sense of the impossible unity is felt as a kind of bewilderment or wonder. I must place 'impossible' in scare quotes because the wholeness manifest in the dynamic belonging-together of the contingent and the necessary is manifestly *not* impossible to experience, even if the conjunction seems to have the character of a logical impossibility. The experience of the unity that seems both contingent and necessary is just another way to speak about the uncanny existential encounter with myself that I have been describing. Impossibility pertains to this unity only insofar as the unity seems to be a logical impossibility. But a dynamic being-together of the possible and the necessary can be felt in a mode of being in which *I am not there*. This kind of not being there may occasionally and explicitly occur and is marked by what I have been calling the mood of the familiar-strange.

Love, or at least erotic attachment, is one name that has been given to the miracle of the 'impossible' unity that belongs to what is contingent and yet could not be otherwise. Death is another.

1.4

Sensation is not well calibrated. Pain. I cannot remember if it hurt more to break my foot when I was thirty-three or my hand at forty-one. I know which of these accidents was more serious. I remember the costs; but I cannot compare the experiences as to which hurt more. Anger is just as rough in marking some of the big differences between the situations in which anger obtains. Erotic desire is no better. Eros may have a priority over other moods or emotions – and I think it does – but not because it is any more discerning than other feelings or moods. Eros is always something of an embarrassment.

I am unable to discern the difference in the desire I felt during a one-week romance with a complete stranger in the south of France many years ago and the desire I felt for my wife when we were first courting. It is an embarrassment that erotic desire (which has, at crucial moments, reorganized my life, confused me, lifted me towards heaven and even left me close to despair) cannot or will not honor that one of my lovers has been vastly more important to me than the other. It is shameful that my desire is so blind. I have even thought that every urge that serves or leans towards survival is ultimately an embarrassment, and that every assertion of my right to survive is as shameful as the heroic context has always found it to be. I say this because the heroic is a system of social relations that barely tolerates self-preservation. All the while Eros remains nearly irresistible.

I am familiar with every inch of her: her body, her response to my touch, her generosity, her hunger and her greed. At times I cannot even tell her arms and legs from my own. But in most of my erotic activity, which is to say almost always, I do tell our limbs apart and I have not mixed myself up with my lover. I seem to operate her body, as she does mine, for the sake of giving and receiving pleasure. From time to time, I fall into the unified activity of lovemaking that is free from thought and so free from fantasy. This selfless erotic bonding is a miraculous occurrence. Despite my intense, even overwhelming familiarity with her, in the uncanny emergence of the 'I' that may happen in the midst of a fully unified act of lovemaking – an emergence that is inevitable – there also manifests an unbridgeable gap: I recognize that I cannot be certain that she feels about me as I do about her.

Not only is it impossible for me to be certain about how she feels about me, Eros seems to demand that I *should not* be certain about her love. In dissolving into her, I find that I have completely surrendered to uncertainty; to be defeated by Eros is not merely *to be uncertain*. The ultimate defeat is to want to be uncertain. Caught up in the erotic, I want to give freely, which means foregoing expectation of return. It is crucial to notice and to remember that the love of one's beloved is not a small thing to put in play: wars have been started over less. In being taken by Eros, I am delivered to a certain kind of freedom. Under erotic unity, I am free to let go of my efforts to secure myself from my uncertainty concerning the object of my desire and relish my vulnerability to the pure dynamism of the circumstances in which I live. 'I' am not there at all. Eros makes possible a choice that is perhaps always available to me even if this choice is precisely the one I normally shun. For the most part, I endeavor to minimize my exposure to the vicissitudes of my needs and desires and even congratulate myself for making myself and my loved ones as secure against chance as I am able. But in the pull of the mind-bending mass that constitutes erotic attraction, I *may* be drawn towards my vulnerability to her, surrendered to the uncertainty that is somehow natural about how it is I am to presume upon her love for me. It happens that my uncertainty and vulnerability appear as desirable.

Even if desire has long been said capable of desiring only what it lacks (that erotic desire is at bottom negative), I want to say that Eros is ultimately not privative. It arises out of the blankness of selflessness that relishes its own ignorance. I am in love with her not because I trust her. I do not seek to put myself at risk. I am not the agent in any of this. In the heat of erotic desire, I trust her because I am in love with her. Only in the emergence of the 'I' from the all-too-rare unity of erotic passion do I explicitly notice that the lack I desire is she; she is the lack (of certainty) I want. This insight is always uncanny even if it is also obvious (at least in a certain register). Eros frees in that it allows. Eros allows me to want to be uncertain and to crave being vulnerable to her. Eros does this against almost all reason, and so it does not insist that the nature of this desire become explicit. Mostly, the explicitness of my vulnerability does not obtain.

It is possible for me to believe that the lack desired by Eros is not the negation or the loss of something I want or need, not because I can figure Eros out or because I can calculate that there is not actually a loss incurred in desiring my own uncertainty, but for two related reasons. First, my desire for the uncertainty of her love is attested in the fact that I am actually driven to bind myself erotically to the one I love. Second, the nature of this drive has, from time to time, been made explicit to me in a direct encounter with the uncanny fact that I can never be sure her love is mine. I experience what I cannot calculate when I want to be in love. And I want to be in love, not because it feels worse, but because it feels better (to be uncertain and vulnerable).

In speaking about wanting to be vulnerable, I have been speaking about a state of being, a kind of unity that is selfless, that exists at the extreme end of passion where erotic attachment is indistinguishable from erotic un-attachment. Despite the natural wholesomeness of erotic union, I am unable to profit from our lovemaking because I am unable to sustain myself within the openness that Eros both promises and demands. Passions cool as suddenly as they flare. Erotic attachment, like every other mood, is not only impermanent but also mostly beyond my control. Perhaps there is a more reliable way to embrace my vulnerability and uncertainty? Not only the uncertainty of her love but all the uncertainty that surrounds the business of living? Perhaps not. But I do know that the possibility of desiring vulnerability and uncertainty can actually happen. I have experienced 'wanting to be uncertain' and 'wanting to be vulnerable,' no matter how fleeting or how incomprehensible these desires may have been. Erotic love in its fullest form is existentially pleasurable even as it takes its bearings from one of the strongest physical imperatives that may call to the human spirit. Such pleasure comes for free and is fleeting. Unable to maintain a tolerance for uncertainty – except when opened up out of unity in the heat and humidity of erotic attraction – perhaps I should let go of too much lovemaking and get back to work? It seems that I should get back to my study, sit at my desk and work through the morning.

1.5

Death is another name for the unity or belonging together between the possible and the necessary. Death is contingent. I might die, but I do not know when. It is necessary because I must die. I cannot escape this possibility and, in this way, as something necessary and possible, as ultimate, death is unlike other possibilities I have.

Death is not like being a father. I became a father. My brother did not. It was possible for me to be a father. The very fact that death is mine prohibits me from taking it up in the same way I inhabit the possibility of fatherhood. If I achieve death, I am manifestly not there. I cannot reach far enough to touch my death. It is not even clear what I mean when I speak of my death, if I mean it in the sense of its being mine. Does not 'my death' belong more to others – the ones left behind – than myself? Death keeps me from the experience of my death because there is no moment at which I am dead now. As soon as I am dead, I am no more. Necessarily beyond my experience, the death of my body is not mine as other possibilities are mine to inhabit. Experientially speaking, my death seems to be as impossible as it is certain. It is not clear how death is mine if death itself makes it impossible for me to be there for it.

Neither can I get past the fact that my death seems to be inevitable or that it really seems to be mine. I do not believe my death is not mine or that my death cannot really affect me even if I know otherwise. Death has a kind of availability that is different from the availability that belongs to logical possibility. Logical possibility is both contingent and not necessary, whereas death seems to bind the contingent to the necessary. To say my death is locked away from me in the future and that it is certain to be sprung on me at some time fails to do justice to the sense in which my death looms for me at all times. Death haunts me in its absence. Time, in my usual understanding of it, does not seem to be able to contain the unity of death's possibility and its necessity. I cannot get past my finitude no matter how much or how loudly I declare that I am not dead now or that death will never really be mine. Death is never here now yet is nevertheless always about.

The indeterminacy of my certain death suggests that my death, in some manner or other, is and has always been here with me from the beginning. Death seems to be a way in which I am not here. What if I only think I understand what being in the mode of not being here means? Maybe death is not just a mass of stinking flesh? Because death is always around anyway, it must have some way to be that is not identical to the death of my body. If death is mine in its persistent absence, then it might be possible for me to experience this modality of death much as I have experienced not being here in the uncanny emergence of myself from the dreamless and thoughtless engagement I have had (from time to time) with my activity? I might even find that I am capable of desiring death not as the end of body but in explicitly taking up the body's way to be in the same strange way in which I have desired the uncertainty of my lover's love and my own vulnerability in the context of erotic unity. But such hopes and aspirations remain mostly speculative or at least somewhat out of reach in that I do not seem to be able to enact at will the sense of contingency that belongs to the familiar-strange.

1.6

Why do I bother to write about feeling weird or strange? What is important about this sense of the familiar-strange? Much as I do when I suffer *déjà vu*, I am likely to acknowledge the uncanny feeling that belongs to an encounter with myself and then, quite sensibly, get on with my life. I take note of the familiar-strange manifestation of myself to myself and pass on. And why not? These moments in which I find myself within the pull of the familiar and the strange are notable but they seem to have no practical force at all. Having been caught up in the experience of the strange unity of the possible and the necessary, having somehow managed to stumble over and past the fences of language and antinomy, I find, if I check, that I have just tasted something very much like the real and stumbled upon what feels like the truth.

The truth. Any contact with the real or the true is compelling to me in the face of a life that has always been more difficult than I expected it to be. Practically speaking, my life has been a sequence of promises, disappointments, failures and achievements. I take myself to win and to lose. Moreover, my life is apparently building madly its elaborate past for the grave. In the cold draft that flows from the certainty of a death outstanding, the meaning of my existence is threatened. Whatever this life of mine is, it is surely bound up in activity and meaning. Activity requires an end to be what it is. Activity has no meaning without a *telos* towards which it reaches. If life is an activity, the *telos* of life seems to be death. What sort of meaning belongs to this ultimate end? Death seems to threaten meaning in the same manner in which death threatens life: utterly. To live without meaning is to despair. But the despair that belongs to living with the indefinite and yet certain *telos* (of death), does not feel as absolute or as final as I calculate it to be. How despairing am I when I walk my dogs? What does it really mean to forget death and live? I cannot (because I do not) accept that life is as meaningless as it adds up to be – and not because I know something about life that I am not sharing with you. I simply do not *believe* my life has no meaning and, at the same time, I do not know why. In considering my life, it seems as if I have always just forgotten something.

In encountering myself in childhood or in hunting or fishing, I sometimes remember myself in a way that is altogether unlike other modes of recollection with which I have experience. I remember myself as emerging from a certain mode of not being there and so as something other or something more than a past that is failing into the future. This something other is an indefinite contact with something more than my opinions, understandings, my dreams, hopes, accomplishments and failures. In the uncanny experience of self-encounter I sense that I am more than an unfinished existence that must struggle with despair.

Two

2.0

Sixty-five years ago my father and grandfather went for a walk on one of the mountains that form the spine of the Olympic peninsula. They hiked most of the day. As it began to get dark, my father was told they were lost and would be spending the night on the mountain. When you are lost it is important not to become too cold, too tired or more lost than you already are. It is better to wait for the light of day. My grandfather in his savage familiarity with wild places curled up and fell asleep under a tree. He slept the whole night through. My father hardly closed his eyes. The air was cool and damp. He was hungry. But the worst by far was that his fear flared with every creak and groan of the northern rain forest. A few minutes before the sky began to brighten, my grandfather woke, stretched and led his son not more than a quarter mile to the car parked on the side of a fire road. My father was fourteen and his father sixty-five.

A little Eskimo boy had been flown in from Alaska for some sort of operation; after he was taken off his IV he seemed healthy but would not eat. The staff tried everything. He spoke no English. When my mother came on duty, she sent one of the aides down to the market for fresh mackerel. She offered the fish whole and raw. The boy devoured it. My father's father adored my mother. I was born in his house and we lived with him until I was six months old. At that time, my father, twenty-five, was a graduate student and my mother, twenty-three, the supervising nurse on the night shift at a pediatric hospital in Seattle.

Even if my father did not, my mother wanted her own household. Granddad bought us a little place near a lake just outside of town. I have seen a picture of it. Before I was three, that house was sold and we were living in New York. A few years later, we moved back to Seattle. I turned five in a little house tucked into the hills over the city-center and we were back in

New York before I was six. My grandfather visited us in New York for a week a few months before he died – I was seven. He took pictures of us in the Washington Square Mews.

He took beautiful photographs: the view of the sound from the living room; the garden in deep snow taken in the half-light during a heavy fall. He had a collection of ancient Leica cameras and light meters my father could never properly operate. Granddad took our baby pictures: my brother and I playing in the gladiolas and snapdragons of his garden tumbling down the hillside in terraces below Magnolia Boulevard. I caught bees when they crawled into the snapdragons and kept them in jars.

My memory of grandfather's house in Seattle is sketchy. I have a sense of the alley out back, the stairs down to the kitchen, the living room with its Victorian sofas of mahogany and complicated fabric, woven carpets. I have a strong impression of the view of Puget Sound from the living room – but I cannot really sort out whether the view through the long wall of plate glass is an original impression or a conflation of photographic images I have seen from early childhood. Memory. I am sure I don't have an original impression of my grandfather's bedroom. I was never in the room. But I do have an image of it in my head. There are stacks of yellowing newspapers and magazines floor to ceiling bound in string through which paths allowed one to move about the room. The picture I have of his bedroom belongs to my own imagination. I learned about his bedroom from stories. I was told that his wife, a woman I called her "grandma" only after his death, had her own room. He slept on a sun porch filled with enormous jade plants that had to be cut down in order to move them off after his death. I have lived long enough to know that not all my memories coincide with the memories of others who were there. Such differences may be beyond resolution. Like Hesiod's muse, the past sometimes speaks truth and at other times falsehood, and man is powerless to discern the difference. It is the nature of the past to be unreliable and incomplete.

A few months before my fifth birthday, I climbed down the back stair in the dark and went into the kitchen where I found my grandfather preparing his breakfast: a concoction of who-knows-what in what must have been one of the first blenders sold in America. After a massive coronary at forty-eight, my grandfather changed his life. He became interested in whole grains, wheat grass, alfalfa tea and black strap molasses. This particular morning, he poured out his drink, vile to behold, drank it and then picked up an orange. With a knife too sharp for a little boy to touch, he began sweeping away the skin in one long continuous peel. He must have noticed how carefully I was watching him. He handed me the peel. I put it back together and formed an empty ball. Then he put the knife in one of my hands and an orange in the other. Did he speak to me? I tried to keep the knife steady. The peel broke. He gave me another orange and then a pile of apples. One by one I bared the fruit to its flesh long past any desire to eat.

Because he was willing to teach me how to use a knife, to allow me to hold it in my hand and cut the fruit or my fingers as I would, he also took me fishing. I can barely make out the impression of the splintered wood of a rough and uneven little dock standing out into a pond. There is the shadow-presence of someone else in my thought. I was catching trout. Somewhere along the line – too excited to speak or even quite notice – I wet my pants. Too many fish and it was raining. I am not sure when I discovered that the pond was stocked. I believe my father told me but I do not remember. It seemed at the time as if I might have walked on the surface of that pond there were so many fish – a mass of gulping faces staring up at me through the slick surface reflecting the darkness of the sky. And it occurs to me now – and for the first time – that pond was probably not open to the public. The shadow-presence was someone my grandfather knew – the owner or the caretaker of the fishery.

I could smell the pee in my trousers when I got in the car and was embarrassed. Granddad did not notice. Brown corduroy trousers. Once upon a time there was a bedspread made out of the same material. I have a memory of the feel of the material against my face. Homecoming with granddad and all those fish was a little hectic. I was soaking wet. My father produced a camera with a flash. I was mostly overwhelmed but in the picture I am smiling. I didn't understand what it meant to catch so many fish. Only once again, just a few years ago, fly-fishing with my father-in-law in the ocean off Catalina when we got into a huge school of bonita, did I ever catch so many fish in such a short time. Somewhere there is a picture of me standing in the kitchen in my yellow rain coat, black rain boots and brown corduroy trousers with a string of trout a yard long. Like the tiny shard of glass from the kitchen floor that has worked its way into the ball of my foot, a shard I sometimes feel but never find, I do not remember the sound of my grandfather's voice.

2.1

At just over ten thousand feet, Horsefly is the highest point on the Uncompahgre Plateau. The long narrow ranch cuts across the lower reaches of the mountain. To the east, a ridge of fourteen-thousand-foot peaks obstructs the sun for almost an hour after dawn breaks. A ragged wall of rock and snow. Pure Colorado. I drove up to Ridgeway from Los Angeles in about eighteen hours, found the ranch, worked the locks and gates with a flashlight and got to sleep by midnight. On Election Day, I killed an elk in the timber.

It is commonly said that elk are everywhere and nowhere. I hunted the south end of the ranch for a full three days without seeing an elk or any fresh sign. On the fourth morning, pre-dawn, I was in my truck crawling along the ranch road when I spotted tracks of a good sized group in the wash of the headlights. I was excited. The elk were up wind from the road. The herd of perhaps thirty or forty animals had pushed across the road sometime during the night, grazed in the pasture next to the ranch headquarters and then moved into the several thousand acres in timber that covered most of the middle sections of the ranch. I waited in the truck. A half hour before dawn – the start of legal shooting hours – I got out. There is no point looking for elk in the dark. If I should have run into them before I was able to shoot them, there would have been a mad crashing of big shapes and then they would have moved – maybe twenty miles before they stop. Look for elk with a rifle. Just before the sun came up, I started out straight into the wind. Elk are seldom found downwind.

Once I entered into the forest of mixed pine and aspen, I moved slowly and deliberately behind the herd. I expected the elk to be spread out all though the well-spaced trees grazing and quiescent. But they might have been anywhere. At ten o'clock in the morning, I walked right up on a cow resting under a group of small pines. She startled me. It had taken me more than three hours to cover the last mile – one foot in front of the other. How had I not seen her before? How had she not seen me? When I saw the cow, she was no more than sixty yards away lying in the snow under a copse of stunted pine. If one moves very slowly and carefully, keeping one's face into the wind, it is not terribly difficult to walk up on elk. I froze and then slowly found my way to the ground. She was casually chewing and looking about. I watched her for about fifteen minutes with my rifle across my knees. The light air was backing. She must have winded me. With moderate urgency the old cow continued to sample the air as she found her legs. She had her nose high in the breeze. She wasn't panicked. Spooked, elk bolt and are gone in seconds. I suspect she only had a whiff of me and could not really tell where I was – all she knew was there was a human somewhere. The rest of the herd condensed from the shadows, fell in behind her and all of them moved off at a trot in single file. The line of elk strung out behind the cow wound though the trees and bushes then crossed the draw moving smartly up the hillside rising gently to the north. They were gone in a moment. I continued to sit still and moved my eyes back into the wind. I continued to search out the deepness of the trees and shadow. Sometimes a bull will hang back concealed. A big bull has also learned when not to move.

I remained still for twenty minutes or so, rose and cautiously walked over to where the cow had lain on the ground. Exploring the area, I studied her tracks and the tracks left by the herd. Tracks point more and less explicitly to ways in which the world has been. In following tracks, I tried to read how it happened, the whole of it. The narrative gets richer as I am able to pay more attention, not only to the tracks themselves – how each is made, its depth, the condition of the track wall – but also what is around the tracks. In paying attention to the marks of the animal, I fall into the world of the elk. Questions foster answers that foster more questions. What were these creatures doing here – sleeping, feeding or just moving through? Did an animal break that branch or bend down that grass? Why were they moving in this direction and not another? Were they going somewhere specific or just wandering? What is ahead of them and what is behind? By studying the tracks of animals I have observed, I have learned about some of the differences in the tracks between an animal that is grazing, animals that are simply moving through on their way to somewhere else, and elk that are spooked.

The ground was patchy with snow where I had first seen the cow. I found her impression. All around her were the tracks of the rest of the herd grazing through the light snow. Many of these marks looked like comets with long tails. Elk graze with their noses to the ground and also they do not pick up their feet much at all. Not only do they leave the tracks of their noses sliding across the ground, they tend to set a hoof and then as they move on from that spot lightly drag the edge of that same hoof across the surface of the ground before picking it up in order to set it down flat again to bear their weight. When elk trot they are reasonably clean stepping. When elk run the tracks get deeper and wider. Running, the cloven hooves of these large and powerful ruminants splay as they hit the ground. When they pick up their feet again, the hooves contract, grab and so toss chunks of snow or mud in their wake. I find the tracks of running elk in groups of four at least fifteen feet apart, sometimes further.

Tracking is like reading a text. When I read a book, I am already leaning in the direction the sentence is going. What this means is that in following what is being said, I am leading the text. In the same way I pick up a glass within the possibility of drinking water, in being there with what is being said between us, I have already reached out ahead of the words spoken in the direction in which we are going. It is only because I do not distinguish myself from what is being said or who is saying it when I read or speak that it is possible to move along with the words on the page. Without leaning into the future the world does not appear: everything that shows up for me shows up as having been. Surprise is created when the world turns up otherwise than I understood the world to be. Surprise is only possible because, in reading text or in tracking an animal, I anticipate.

There are obvious differences between reading tracks and a book – the intention of the author to communicate something at least seems to be one of the most important differences – but both kinds of reading, books and animal tracks, have to do with and entering into and falling from the flow of what is being read. One moves with the text or the tracks until one is stopped. Something has shown up as unintelligible. At that place it is necessary to consider, to look about for clues, to reconstruct the situation anew, attempting to draw upon the availability of the world in which the texts or the tracks make sense. One is always inclined forward in following an animal in the field even if there are different modes of being ahead of what is happening. Not every kind of anticipation makes possible surprise.

It takes a story to track an animal, not just marks on the ground. The tracks I do not immediately see are nevertheless still there. It is a method of tracking to find each one. Sometimes I must calculate where the next track should be and look there. To calculate is another mode in which one looks ahead. I have already started to speculate about, or fall into a sense of, what the animal is doing. It is browsing and grazing under the snow. In trying to find every track, I fall into the rhythm and gait of the beast. I have read that certain Apache scouts were able to track ants moving over rock. The rocks apparently have a thin covering of dust and if one looks closely enough one may be able to find the disruptions in the dust film. I don't know if I believe everything I have read about the Apache tracker, but it is a fact that the more I understand about the animals I am following, the richer my understanding will be of what the particular animal was doing when it made the marks I follow. Not much may mean a lot. Tracking is about moving at the right speed – that speed seems always to be slower.

A heavy bull with a big rack of horn sometimes leaves a dewclaw mark at the back of his track if he is not moving too quickly. Because of his weight his whole foot is pressed down. But I was not looking for a big bull. I was looking for any bull. Any antlered animal with four points on either side was legal and would fill out my tag. I hoped I might come across a young bull moving with the cows or perhaps in a small group of other bulls. Mature bulls, the ones that have won the right to breed, and won that right with their large and impressive antlers, pretty much disappear. I don't believe there were any on the ranch. But who knows?

The big mature males tend to be either where they cannot be legally hunted or tucked up in special hiding places way out of the way. A big bull sometimes waits in his 'nest' for rifle season to end. A few years ago, while hunting chukar in Eastern Oregon at the tail end of deer season, I came across a big mule deer buck up on the very top of the highest hill in the area. He was a spectacular buck: a five by five with huge heavy bases and a lot of separation. When I thought about it, I realized he knew I was there long before I saw him. I never really had much of a shot had I been trying to kill him. After a moment, it occurred to me why he was up there on that little top. He liked to keep track of who his visitors were. I looked around and could see by the myriad of his big tracks and abundance of scat that he had been on that hill top quite a while. Something similar happens with bull elk. Rifle season begins right after the rut. After the rut the bulls, at least the big ones, and any bull that is going to get big, seem to move to a hidden place: the end of a canyon with a back door or a thick stand of pine of no more than a few acres that provides some kind of advantage. Near some kind of water source, they may remain as long as six weeks or so, exhausting the food supply – which just happens to exhaust the hunting season. By staying put and not moving, the bull leaves no tracks to his hiding place. In most of the mountain areas, a trophy bull in his nest cannot be tracked, unless one were to happen upon his tracks within a couple of days of him settling into his hiding spot or discover his path to water. And if I were simply to stumble onto a bull nest, I would have to do so in such a way that I would not bust him out of it. The wind is so likely to give me away. To hunt these animals, one has to guess where the bull is going to be, and then make an approach on that spot that has carefully taken into consideration the wind. Anticipation. One hunts the possibility of the bull, and so, particularly as a beginner, I often find I have been stalking dreams or ghosts.

A strong steady breeze that keeps your scent well behind you is best. A weak wind, in which the air backs and eddies, is difficult to hunt in because it is constantly changing direction and if you do not keep your face into the wind and your scent behind, you will never see or hear an elk. I pay attention only to the wind. I don't bother with scent-masking technology. I don't use scentlock or cover scents. Scentlock is the name of a clothing system that involves special materials, rubber cuffs and activated charcoal inserts. It is designed to trap your scent inside a suit. But what you are wearing or how you smell seems always to be trumped by the direction of the wind. An old timer famous for killing big deer once remarked about my scentlock gear, "if the wind is wrong it doesn't matter and if the wind is right it doesn't matter." And so I didn't try to follow the herd as they had moved more or less down wind from me.

Eleven o'clock. I had kept along the big draw I had been working all morning. In places I could see nearly five hundred yards through the scattered trees. If I were able to gain a rest for the rifle, I felt sure I could make a fairly long shot. I was carrying a slightly customized Winchester model 70 chambered in .338 magnum, topped with a high-end adjustable scope from 1.5× through 6× power. I had started using a range finder a couple of years before. Even when I was practicing regularly at guessing ranges, I found I was off by large factors from time to time – particularly at longer distances. Distance is different in the timber or in a pasture or looking down a steep incline. Moving along the edge of the timber up the draw from tree to tree, I was starting to lose some of my concentration. I caught myself daydreaming here and there and would stop and try again to clear my head and bring my attention to the timber in which I was hunting. I smelled the elk before I saw them.

Elk stink. I do not have much of a nose and even I can smell them. When I saw the elk a few minutes later, they were just upwind of me moving along smartly from left to right in a single thread. The closest was probably 150 yards away. If I waited, the group would pass a little closer. I sat down to gain a rest for my rifle. Placing my elbows resting on my knees to steady my shot, I was running out of time. Breath. There was a group of young bulls in behind the cows. I was spotting the elk through the riflescope as they moved by. I shouldn't do that. I should use binoculars – don't point a rifle at anything you do not intend to kill – but, in as close as I was to the elk and with the elk moving as fast as they were, I was either going to find my bull through the riflescope or I wasn't going to get a shot at him at all. The elk were trotting with their noses up and their heads tilted back looking almost comic. I was pretty sure they had winded me before I had seen them and were leaving the area. Like the cow I had seen an hour before, these elk were not panicked, they just did not know quite where I was.

My rifle is zeroed at two hundred yards. With a 250-grain bullet, the rifle shoots 1.7 inches high at one hundred yards. I am not that well calibrated. The elk had closed my position and were now about a hundred yards off. There seemed to be some legal animals in the group. I started counting points. One bull had four on each side. The one at the end seemed the biggest. I would wait. They were moving a little faster now. One, two, three, four: yes, that little bull is more than legal. I let out half my breath and held it. I could barely feel my pulse. Swinging the rifle as smoothly as I was able, I placed the cross hairs just behind the front leg in the middle of his chest and began to squeeze the trigger. I hardly felt the massive recoil. He went down. The first shot took him clear off his feet. I was pretty sure the shot was a fatal but I did not want him to get up. I worked the bolt and chambered another round. He was trying to collect his feet under him without much success. I steadied the rifle on my knees. I still didn't have time to use the range finder and guessed he was one hundred yards away. I put the crosshairs right on the top of his back, at the base of the neck and fired. I could hear the thud of the bullet. He did not try to get up again.

I gave him twenty minutes to die, and marked the time by my watch. I had been very cool up until that moment, but after he lay there I started to get excited and had to remind myself to be careful. If I come up on him before he is dead, he might bolt. It is amazing how far a mortally wounded elk will run. They are very tough animals. Last year, a friend shot a cow with a fast .30 caliber round from a little too far away. The 180-grain bullet hit her in the chest, got good penetration and the bullet fully expanded, as it should. But traveling as far as it did, the bullet shed a good deal of its energy and consequently the shock value was not as great as it would have been at closer range. Nevertheless, we saw a lot of damage when we cut her open. The cow had run off despite a collapsed lung and a lot of bleeding. We were up all night looking for her and didn't find her until the next morning. She was very weak but still alive.

Twenty minutes later, the bull I had shot lay still. I had already chambered a fresh round: safety on; thumb on the safety; pull the rifle into your shoulder; level it at his chest. I started to come up on him on step at a time. He was over on his side with his head turned awkwardly between his forelegs. His antlers were rolled slightly to one side. He was bigger than I had first thought: a very symmetrical 'five by five' rack (five points on each side). A good-looking animal, he was probably two, maybe even three years old. Elk have miniature tusks inside their mouths called ivories and are the most reliable gauge for guessing age. He was not moving. At ten feet, he looked dead, but a six or seven hundred pound animal getting onto its feet can be more than startling. I approached the bull as mindfully as I was able and lightly touched the tip of the rifle barrel to his eye. He neither blinked nor stirred.

2.2

Why do Americans hunt? If I should be asked this question now, I would answer that we hunt mostly because we do, because we have already done so, because our fathers or our grandfathers hunted, and that we loved them or we hated them. We hunt because hunting is one way in which what has been handed down is manifest. Before I considered hunting, I would have said hunting was instinctual. At the most essential level, I would have presumed that the urge to hunt was bound up with satisfaction or pleasure. I understand that these two ways of answering the question are not mutually exclusive. Both make a claim. A real question is never exhausted by its answer, just as every interpretation is always inadequate to the creation it seeks to express. But my work in these pages was not prompted by a question – not right away. I was not asked why we hunt or even why I hunt, even if these questions have subsequently come up.

I was living with my new wife in a very pleasant working-class neighborhood of Los Angeles. We had a cute house, a broken view of the harbor and were still looking for what was going to direct our marriage. As has been my habit from early childhood, I got up before dawn one morning. I was sleepy and felt especially middle-aged. When I had gone to bed the previous night, my grandfather had not been on my mind. My grandfather had been dead for more than twenty years before I killed my first animal, eleven years in the ground before I bought my first gun.

Standing at the island in the middle of our kitchen in San Pedro, I found myself caught in an uncanny sense of repetition. To remember is also to re-member in the sense of bringing back to life – perhaps aping the Egyptian goddess who put her dismembered brother Osiris back together again and brought him to life. I remembered being four years old, and finding my grandfather in his kitchen doing precisely what I was doing at that very moment. The repetition felt something like *déjà vu*, but not quite. *Déjà vu* never seems to have consequences. I was caught in a different sense of repetition. It was not that that which was before me was being repeated, I was myself the repetition and there were immediate consequences. I was my grandfather that morning. He had showed up to me as who I was, and of course also who I was not. I was struck by the very odd sense that I was a hunter simply because he had taught me to peel an orange when I was not quite five years old.

2.3

I am capable of imagining the past as perfect or complete, but I remember it otherwise. To remember is to re-experience, and so to experience anew. To remember is to raise the dead. A perfect past is the object about which history is written. Strangely, it does not seem to matter much to me that such an objectified past is not like other objects. I know where my teacup is kept, but I have no idea where to find the past. It does not even seem to be 'in time,' which has necessarily passed it by. I only hear tell of the past. All that can be experienced is subject to change and so to decay. The perfected past does not decay. It cannot be remembered. It can only be dreamed.

The past and its history are not synonymous. The difference is expressed in saying that history changes, not the past. The perfected past is taken to be both complete and fixed. What we know about it is what changes. History, like a science, remains open to revision in its hopeless struggle to describe the past. The perfected past is an idea.

In Greek, *the idea of something* (*eidos*) is etymologically related to *the look of it*. Originally an idea seems to have had a verbal sense. How something looks is enacted by a concept or an idea. The concept is taken as that which gathers together acci-dents. But a concept as that activity which gathers together is as misbehaved as language. You know, irony. Language so often says more than was meant. It has been suggested that the look of some particular entity is what gives me that entity, but this is not something merely theoretic. I fell in love with the look of my first wife when I was thirteen years old. I fell in love with her eidos. Of course more happened after that. A great deal more, but that is how it began. I walked into the living room of my new friend from school, her younger brother, and there she was six inches taller than I, and more beautiful than Helen.

Likewise, I know my dog when I see him. I do not look at a mass of details and then assemble the data into my dog. In speaking of knowing in the sense of recognizing, what is spoken about is a kind of understanding. When I say that I understand something I am saying that I have some kind of familiarity with that something. In a funny way then, it is my understanding of how things go that allows what is to be as it is. In allowing something to be as it is, that something shows up as given.

It is not altogether uncommon to imagine death as carrying one beyond life and all possible (earthly) experience. The place to which one is carried after death is transcendent, and a place to which I have no current access. Nevertheless, I find that I do reach death directly in some of the ways in which I actually come to grips with it. Death in some sense is not completely beyond my experience. Death can be here for me in the mode of my own impending absence. I am not speaking of a theoretic or logical absence, for such an absence is never here or there for anyone. I am referring to the palpable absence of myself that is the condition for the experience of self-encounter. Death, not as the death of the body, but as the penumbrae about my existence, the darkness over my own origin, is actually and explicitly encountered in the absence from which I sometimes emerge into that familiar-strange encounter with myself that is always happening for the first time again. When my mortality is explicitly manifest as a kind of phenomenal finitude, why can I not say that death has been felt?

God has been taken to be an idea: the transcendent source of all that is. But for the believer, God is merely an idea only for the non-believer. The believer says that the non-believer would believe if he would open his heart to God. The philosopher and the scientist each tries to open his own eyes. The believer says he has direct contact with God. He tells us God cannot be conceptually grasped, that God is a personal god (the origin of my experience) and can manifest as such. God may belong, in part and in a way that is difficult to speak about, to experience. Unfortunately, I must offer the phenomenal experience of God on hearsay. I do not claim the experience for myself. I include this experience because I find that not only do I admire the believer, but also that, unaccountably, I myself believe that there are and have been persons to whom God has been known. I am unwilling to say such experiences have been merely subjective and I do not have much reason for my disinclination.

Together with the ideal past, the imagined past that is complete and unchanging, there is the past that may be experienced. I may at some moment remember the past. I might encounter myself inhabiting an explicit possibility that has been handed down to me from the past, and, in so doing, encounter myself as another. I have done so. Like death and God, the past is also phenomenal. The hopelessness of history to exhaust the past depends on the fact that we actually do encounter the past. The ideal always depends on the phenomenal, even when it has forgotten why. Today, science still sleeps in the cradle of the phenomenal but sometimes dreams of overthrowing the tyranny of experience.

Unlike my idea of the past as the object of history complete and unchanging, the past I talk about when asked to consider what the past might be, the past I deal with seems to be simply my understanding of what has happened. The past *is* the story I am caught in and nothing besides. To the extent that I do not believe or trust some particular story I know – such is the extent to which that story does not count as the past. I say it might have happened that way, or simply I don't know what happened. That the past is my understanding of the past does nothing to weaken the force of the past, does nothing to make it merely theoretical. Rather, the fact that the past I deal with is a collection of stories that may or may not be consistent, says something about the power and originality of narrative. My understanding of how things go is given by a narrative and is, in its very nature, not under my control. Even if the past is a story, I do not get to make up history. The past is given by its history and now, despite my sense of the past in its beforeness, and so in its inaccessibility, I cannot tell history from the past it describes. When history changes because of certain discoveries or insights that befall me, so does my past. When the past changes, I change right along with it. When I discover that I was disliked in high school or loved in college, the way in which I am is no longer the way in which I once was. *Who I am* has changed. That the past can change necessarily throws all my ideas about time into disarray.

2.4

Toward the end of his life, my father would visit me in California where I had moved for the sake of learning to write poems. In the course of working on them, I noticed I was inordinately interested in my grandfather. He was terribly important to me and yet, in a very real sense, I hardly knew him. I lightheartedly mentioned my fixation to my father. I suppose I was expecting to initiate some sort of self-deprecating banter with my father about how silly I was. I doubt I was really thinking much past the surface of my comment. But there was no banter and nothing lighthearted. My father simply said he was not at all surprised by my attachment to my grandfather. I was surprised and asked why he wasn't. He elaborated: your grandfather thought you were perfect. I believed him in an objective way. It seemed possible. I had seen it in my own life. My mother had felt my children were perfect. But when I asked my father exactly what he meant, he asked me if I were able to remember how hard he, my father, had been on me when I was a little boy. He said this in a completely matter-of-fact manner that emerged from the depth of his own mother's dark brown eyes. Granddad's eyes, as mine are, were a pale blue.

Hector's terrible crest shook along the ridge of his helmet and frightened his son. The child did not know what he was looking at, did not know that the crest was cut from heavy hairs of a horse's tail or that the man before him was even a man, let alone his own father. The boy saw a fiend of flesh and bronze. Had Hector's son seen through the monster to the man and known the armored hero to be his father, the child, nevertheless, would have failed to have recognized that his father's strength, a mere plaything of the gods, would crumble to naught at the gates of their city and that his mother would be led away in slavery; that he, the son and child of the hero, on the point of a spear, would be pitched onto the rocks from the city walls.

When my father explained to me that which was recognizable, I recognized it. He had voiced what I could sense but could not see, and then it was there and it was obvious. My grandfather had loved me. He was powerful. More powerful than my father and so I feared less the slopes of Mount Cithaeron and not *merely* because my grandfather was around, but because he existed at all.

We learned of his passing on a winter weekend in 1959. A telegram. My father was upset but kind. I went with him to a liquor store to cash a check. We were going to leave by train that night for Seattle. I didn't know what to feel. I had to think about my grandfather. I had to imagine being without him forever more. I tried to picture him lying still and dead at the bottom of the stairs. My mother told me the doctor felt granddad's heart attack was so massive he was dead before he reached the ground. I was seven and we had been living on the other side of the country from my grandfather. I was without him being around most of the time anyway. It took time. After a day or so I began to feel the loss of him and then it got much stronger.

2.5

In understanding one's own people as being swept along by public events, even if family history is always a stream that feeds the history of the nation, there is something peculiar about acknowledging the consequences of one's actions, the actions of one's family, as manifest in the history of the world. The private and the public cannot be kept apart. I have always known that my grandfather was in Alaska at the start of the twentieth century, but it has only recently occurred to me that he was there during the famous gold rush. He may even have told my mother that Eskimos find cooked fish revolting. I don't know. My grandmother and grandfather were together in Alaska from 1902 until 1904. Then she went back to Seattle and he stayed in the north until 1907.

A new mining engineer fresh out of college, my grandfather became the superintendent of a gold-mining operation during the five years he spent in Alaska. In support of his duties he spent one or two winters north of the Arctic Circle living with the local Inuit population – living as if he were in the Stone Age, I should expect. Years ago, I read extensively on the subject and character of these northern peoples. Titles such as *The Incredible Eskimo* begin to express the strangeness, even the exotic nature of this extreme land and those who inhabited it. I am full of impressions of European adventurers and missionaries who became interested in these northern people in the first half of the twentieth century. The Inuit are unimaginably tough, their way of life unimaginably fragile.

I was told when I was very young that my grandmother shot a bear as it came into her cabin or tent. Family stories leach into the soil and lie in layers of possibility, out of sight but as available as the aquifers under western farmlands. My father was interested in the dynamics between his mother and father. He was a psychoanalyst. It occurs to me that I was more interested, or just as interested, in shooting a bear. My father always joked that his mother had shot that bear because she thought it was her husband – was that granddad's humor? We would laugh. I'm not sure how funny this is to me right now. She was dead sixteen years before I was born. The rumor is that it was she who spoiled my father to punish my grandfather. So says my father. During the depression she would spontaneously give my father, not yet ten years old, one of the dividend checks on which she lived. This kind of excess in a time of such shortage was deemed disgraceful and drove my grandfather crazy, as it was no doubt designed to do. It is a terrible thing for a child to be used by one parent to punish the other. Myth narrates some of the circumstances in which this happens and offers a few of the reasons why a man's son is sometimes offered up to him – sometimes as a simple aggravation, sometimes as his competitor, sometimes jointed and browned in a savory stew. I came to my understanding of my grandparents' life together from the many stories my father told us, some remarks by my cousin and the few letters and documents that remain. My grandmother died in 1936. My father was eleven.

In the last days of March of 1994, when my father was sick and living suspended between life and death, his mother was the subject of which he preferred to speak until he preferred not to speak at all. Then he would, when he noticed you, simply smile. He was in considerable pain. I remember him being particularly grateful when my wife at that time, a young and pretty woman, would sit next to him. He revisited his childhood loss, not with anxiety, but with a kind of heartfelt equanimity that was touching and utterly beautiful for us, his sons, to behold. He had an aggressive and pernicious cancer, but as long as we were able to keep him medicated, it did not seem to bother him much. He moaned when he felt pain and needed our care. But he needed less and less as the last days wore. Tolstoy explained something of my father's state of mind in *War and Peace* – I am thinking of André's death in the care of Natasha and Mari – how the concerns of the dying are slowly unknit from those of the living and yet continue to understand and honor the fact that these concerns still belong to the living.

2.6

By the time my father was the age I am now, I had pretty much forced him to approve of me. I am only vaguely able to understand that this sort of statement says more about me than him. After he was fifty, I am almost sure he was explicitly aware of the magnitude of my need for his approval even if I was not. Perhaps he was also aware of my need to force it from him? No matter, he gave in willingly and his genuine acceptance of me was his greatest gift to me. I had sought my father's approval with a relentlessness that seemed almost absurd. But once I had secured it and once he had died, the problem of living was still not solved. I found it almost surprising.

My father is dead almost nine years and the sound of his voice has begun to fade as my grandfather's voice faded. The details of his person grow vague: what he smelled like, what he looked like. I cannot reproduce most of his features to myself. There is something of a blank when I try to picture his face. But I do remember the roughness of his beard and the slightness of his hands, and sometimes I am startled by the appearance of a stranger. The face of the cashier or a man that flits across the corner of my eye seems to bear a likeness to his face. I guess that I would recognize him if he were to appear at the door.

When the undertakers came to my house in their black American station wagon pushing their bright folding gurneys of stainless steel that opened up like music stands, they lifted his stiff, cancer-wrung corpse from the hospital bed I had installed in our back bedroom, zipped him up in their black vinyl body bag and rolled him out to the hearse parked in the drive. And then, unbelievably, even outrageously, as if nothing of moment had happened, they drove away. He had become more like firewood than father. I yearned after him down the concrete path and across the lawn. As I watched him go, I rehearsed my loss. I would never be able to call him on the phone; I would never drive out to see him in New Mexico; hear him grind out Bach's partitas on his violin; 'I would never...' reverberated. Drama. I counted the years that remained to me and for the first time measured my life from death.

I knew I had felt this kind of desperate grief before. I first discovered the inconsolable feeling of loss when I wept for my grandfather thirty-seven years earlier. Our train trip through Canada was beautiful. I remember weeping all the way from New York to Seattle and then from Seattle to New York. I wept at his funeral. But I did not weep continuously – it only seems that way and even this sense of continuity is beginning to break up. The assumption of continuity is a trick the devil likes to play. Mostly I am not self-conscious. Mostly I am not there at all. When I claim to be miserable or anxious, these harsh feelings, if I check, always fill less of the day than it feels like they do. I wander about doing this and that with virtually no thought of myself at all. The 'I' fills up far less than I suppose it does. I played on the train. I remember speaking with the other passengers, the observation car, the ruggedness of the mountains, the forests. I was having my first real taste of the same Rocky Mountains in which I would hunt as a middle-aged man.

When my father died I found that I was weeping not merely for the loss of my father because without thought, my grief spilled over into a longing for my grandfather. Quite all at once I wept for him, and so it was revealed to me at that moment that the loss of my grandfather had always been the spring box from which I had always drawn grief. Overflowing this container as well, I soon found I was weeping for my whole dead line *as if* I had known each one. I imagined each of my ancestors in his flesh. I plunged into inconsolability – each of my ancestors drying into the script that formed his name. Each one drying into a line of ink in a genealogical chart, that paper grave which keeps the unknown father in place. I imagined my own death. It occurred to me that when all of my father's sons were dead, so too must he die again. And that there would be no second burial. Those left upon the earth would not, indeed could not, commemorate *my* father. My father would have been as strange to them before as he would be after my death. And with this thought I was released into weeping for the generations, for every mother, every father lost beyond recall – each with hands harsh and gentle by turns, his or her life opening and closing like a door, flexing like the wings of an insect – butterflies in clouds over Canada, over the Great Plains dreaming of Mexico.

2.7

On a recent trip to New York, I happened to be passing through a neighborhood in which I had once lived. Of course, I knew where I was but it was still a surprise to find myself standing outside the black cast iron fence surrounding the swing and slide sets on which I had played as a child. As if bound hand and foot to the spot, I looked about shuffling thin memory until I came back to myself having realized my attention had been completely taken over by a young woman sitting on a bench. She was half reading, half looking on while her toddler flailed about the sand box with his bucket and shovel. And there I was thinking of my own mother. I could almost remember what it felt like to be off in the world with my games and adventures, and yet still feel within the ambit of her reach. An odd sense of my own mortality washed over me an before I could adjust to the fact that the experience had already changed. Perhaps it was the smoothness of her face or the translucence of her skin, but without transition, her appearance no longer carried me to my mother but to the mother of my own children – my first wife at twenty-one or twenty-two. That woman in the park guarding her child, not much more than a girl herself, had within a single moment shown herself both as mother and lover and I desired her twice.

The adolescent is as savage as he is beautiful. Consumed by erotic desire he is always willing to burn the past to the ground for the sake of the future, for he lives at the crisis of his affections, an attachment to his mother, to the home in which he was reared, and his longing for some place and someone of his own. This crisis occurs at the nexus of a shape-change. The body that nourished becomes the body that stimulates. Like Philomela's transmogrification into the songless swallow or Tereus' sudden passage into the hoopoe, hard-beaked and wild, the adolescent does not notice his wings as much as they simply beat the air, for mother and lover are manifestly different and of different kinds. It is only nostalgia that is unable to distinguish a mother long dead from a girl who no longer exists.

2.8

Nostalgia has as little respect for memory as it has for time. My brother reported to me that during a recent stay in Trinidad, his first visit to the island in more than thirty years, as he sailed into the harbor he found himself feeling powerfully nostalgic for a time he knew perfectly well had been one of the most difficult periods of his life. I have experienced this same phenomenon dreaming back to my days in boarding school, which seemed a prison at the time, or certain epochs belonging to each of my marriages. The clanking absurdity of desiring that which lies beyond what can be touched or in any way experienced is ridiculous enough, but that the clamoring of such longings persist fawning on memories that memory itself recalls as burdens to have lived, is a risibility too fragile to comprehend.

The women in Achilleus' shelter weep for Apollo-slain Patroklos. Here the miseries of the captured women blend with the miseries of Achilleus. Achilleus wept for Patroklos, the women wept with him but their thoughts soon turned to their dead brothers, dead fathers, their sisters and mothers bound and led into slavery. Patroklos, whose heavy hands had taken so many lives dear to these captured women, was the agent of the women's current misery and yet he was himself the object of their nostalgia. How could grief be more bittersweet or binding of contrary dispositions?

Grief, in certain important ways, is always the same. It does not matter for whom I weep. Grief searches out an emptiness that is both too hard and too sweet to bear. Grief is monolithic *because* it is so indiscriminate. I have longed into the past: for comfort, for family and for the fullness and heat of the hearth. The abandon with which I have been able to give myself over to my grief astounds me. Truly the work of tears is to wash away pain. But perhaps some pain is best not relieved, or at least not too soon, not before what has been given to be understood by these tears is understood.

Nostalgia was the song the Sirens sang, a song that drew a pilot's attention into the indeterminacy of desire, of what was missing and beyond recall, of what was not, or was no longer. Nostalgia is what drew the pilot's mind from the keel that parts the foaming sea and headlong into desire – a longing for what is beautiful to eye and ear, a longing for home, and for being at home, and yet such feelings can be so thick one is unable to see the impossibility on which a man may wreck and drown.

2.9

All desiring or longing seems to be caught up in some projection of the future. Desire places what is desired before me. I look forward to it. To desire is to want what is missing – to want it someday. In this sense, nostalgia imagines the past in the future, even as it knows it is unattainable. Nostalgia is one way in which the future gets filled up with the past and in this way nostalgic longing is always, though never explicitly, a way of leaning into the future. Such a future, a future that is yet to come is bounded by death – whether I like it or not and whether I think about it or not.

Nostalgic longing seems to be irreconcilable with a certain state of mind in which I might encounter the original nature of my death. To wish for the impossible, to imagine that being at home only happens in the past, is only an idea, is to understand oneself as forever out of place. To long for the impossible is to imagine oneself as immortal. What is impossible, being with no possibility, is death. Impossible desires are as diffident as they are defiant. In nostalgia's blind disregard of death, a fantastical embrace of the impossibility of impossibility, nostalgia denies the proximate nature of death, which is to say selflessness and the nothingness from which I always seem to arise. The incompatibility between nostalgia as a looking backwards and every fearless leaning forward that belongs to the erotic, to completely engaged activity, is usually invisible.

For instance, in one version of the heroic, the possibility of death remains explicit, even as the heroic mood remains essentially nostalgic. The heroic encounter with life in its most complete moment is, like the orgiastic, a unifying experience – the self is absorbed into a kind of war-making that cares nothing for death.

The Helvetii wished to live somewhere else as they were constrained from easily carrying out war with their neighbors because of the topography of their territory. They prepared to move for two years and in the third burned their farms and villages to the ground. They vowed to displace any who stood in the way of their migration. Like the Spartans, they submitted to poverty in exchange for strength in war. The Helvetii literally put their *longing for home* in front of them.

In this way of telling the story, these Celtic people turned the world upside down and let nostalgic longing explicitly look forward. In this way they attempted to cause the future. Nostalgia feeds the kind of courage that is a head-longing into death, the war-rage born out of a longing for relief, for return. The pagan warrior before his enemies recites the names of his forebears and works up a longing to join them in that place which looks very much like a perfected past. He works up a longing to throw himself against the hardness of battle and death, works up a desire for death from the fearlessness that belongs to having embraced the impossible. In the awful heat of war, in the oaths made under the rafters of the feasting halls, one is drawn out of the volatility of one's finitude, drawn from one's fragmented existence to become hardened into the blade by which war is waged. The sense of abandon is orgiastic as it feels overwhelmingly good to be without fear.

The heroic depends on nostalgic longing in a very strange way. It embraces the impossibility of nostalgic desire and takes this impossibility to be coincident with the impossibility of being at all. The hero lives in his war rage in a way that is without duality. The heroic explicitly embraces death as a final return but without ever noticing that nostalgic longing is not dexterous enough to tease apart the possible from the impossible or the bitter from the sweet. The fact that nostalgia sometimes looks longingly back to what was unpleasant to live may be an indication that what is at work in longing for the unobtainable past has simply not been made clear.

2.10

Consciousness dreams the world into pieces. It discovers structure without content and content without structure. To be conscious is to have taken a position, to have imagined oneself apart and separate from that which consciousness has before it. Consciousness is always self-consciousness. In the usual sense of wanting something from which one feels separated, desire belongs to consciousness. To desire gets felt as a reaching from the inside to the outside, as a need that arises to connect oneself to that which presents itself as desired. Consciousness experiences wanting in terms of what is missing. Desire presupposes lack even if it is difficult to understand how is it possible to desire that which I already have.

If consciousness were to be likened to the flickering presence of a star in the heavens, then awareness might be the blackness behind – a blackness so deep and steady as to be unfathomable in its very way to be. Awareness is like the silence manifest in the rustling of grass at dusk when the wind dies and leaves the ears yearning for the horizon. For awareness seems in some sense to be the very condition for there being anything at all. Awareness is kind or *kinding* because it is the very belonging together that is the holding together of all that is. Awareness is the sounds of traffic together with the face of a child crossing the street, the scent of spring coming through the blue of air over the flow of automobiles.

And yet for all its enormity, without a star, without the possibility of a point of view how could awareness even be? Awareness is the *wanting* of the world into being. And yet it is only when consciousness resurrects from the death of self that lack, and so desire, is born. It is only from the separation that belongs to *taking* a point of view that anything can be conceived of as missing.

So desire may not originate in lack at all. Rather it may be that desire has been delivered between the knees of an abundance that is impossible to separate from the world at large. And to know this, to have sighted and then pronounced the unity of all things, to say, "all is one" or "god is love," is merely to have made a noise. Such pronouncements are a sounding brass. For to be able to spell the origin of desire, to express this origin in the word 'love' or 'awareness,' cannot muffle the sound of the iron shoes that trample the heart of every living man. Knowledge of love will not save one from suffering the poverty and aguish of disappointment and loss long associated with Eros – that god whose father was rich and whose mother was poor; the god who at one moment is lounging on lavish couches, and in the next is crouched in a doorway trying to keep out of the wind and rain. Awareness is not a thing said, nor a thing done. Neither can it be over and done. Awareness belongs to, or is origin and origin seems to be nothing more or less than the incessant and mysterious human effort to enact it.

That we suffer the lack of what we desire is a fact. Not a problem. Because on certain days, Eros so overwhelms me with his always unexpected vigor that he is able to free me from my certainty, erase my knowledge of that mystery which hangs about the roots of all that is. Before the god of love I am senseless. Wounded by his arrows consciousness dies. Time fails. Those fences that kept everything from happening at once are suddenly allowed to fall. On such days I might walk by a park in which I once played as a child and find myself at every age. For as I walked away from those black iron pickets, I desired them all: my mother when I was a child, my girlfriend in high school, my young wife, the mother of my sons. For I had fallen in love with that perfect stranger in whose radiant fecundity the world was brought into being again, and for the first time.

Yes, 'again and for the first time,' for *déjà vu* marks the presence of the god as surely as gray heaven accompanies the rain. *Love's not time's fool*, for love unhinges time. One is always in love again and for the first time. And yet the failure of desire to obey either the laws of decency or physics disquiets me. Zeus carried off Europa and put an end to her childhood. Theseus raped Helen as a girl of ten or twelve. And I? What is it that I want to do?

Even as erotic longing begins to dissolve the space between us, I have begun to dream about the future in terms of satisfaction. Even under the sway of what is beautiful, I keep remembering myself. But when I am without a place, when I am in that moment that neither begins nor ends, I am as the wind singing in the rigging – at home everywhere.

Nostalgia longs not only for the ghost of what is no longer possible, what has been safely hidden in time, but something else as well. What this might be I cannot quite grasp. Perhaps it is something forgotten, something that cannot be taken or seen from any point of view – a far richer temporality than any imagination can dream.

And so touched by desire's needs and losses, it is right that when I catch sight of myself, a man falling away from his prime in love with a girl given to another, that I should grieve for all that has passed though my hands – and yet in love with her as I am it seems at once that I have not desired her too much, but too little. For fundamentally to desire enough is to consume every disappointment and undo the very possibility of stupidity. To encounter Eros is to soften into the impossibility of that moment which neither begins nor ends, and in so doing abandon every hope and lean into the future without fear. To be without hope is to be as fearless as only someone in love can be. To be in love is to dive headlong into the rapture of the obvious – that everything is as it should be.

2.11

Neither comfort nor discomfort led Socrates' actions, unless desiring virtue is a comfort or a discomfort. He prepared for his death as casually as if he were getting ready for a nap, making no concession to his impending execution until the hemlock had numbed him to his stomach and his heart began to grow cold. Only then did Socrates bring the conversation to a close and shut his eyes.

Socrates had been debating with friends on his last day, as he would have on any other day. The topic under discussion was apropos as usual: is there or is there not an afterlife? And as was usual, the topic was a question. But no sooner had Socrates closed his eyes in readiness for death, than he opened them up. Asklepios. It was the custom to sacrifice to Asklepios when a person was cured of his ailment. Would Crito be so kind as to sacrifice a cock to Asklepios for him? Why did Socrates remember this courtesy just as death was sweeping over him? Did he feel relief? Is it a relief to have his life's burdens taken away? Could it be that a good man is not afraid to die because living well is so exhausting – like the running of a long and exhilarating race? How much energy does it take to keep the world open with a question? The last act of a man condemned for impiety should be an act of piety. He must thank the god for the medicine that was finally to cure him of life. Irony is almost an aggravation.

A friend is speaking to you on the phone and the next day his wife calls and says through her tears choked-back and flowing that your friend is dead. That is how death comes. My father died. But when I left the room and walked into my own living room, what difference did his death make to me? Had I not seen his dead body, perhaps I might have thought that he was still alive in the back bedroom or, better, alive and well in New Mexico writing poems and playing tennis. But at five o'clock in the morning on April 6, 1994, God forgave him. Why was I inconsolable? My father stopped breathing, my grandfather toppled down a set of stairs, my mother went to sleep and did not wake up.

Other witnesses to Socrates' death have reported that as the jailer mixed the hemlock, Socrates was busy learning to play a new tune on the flute. Socrates did not seem to suffer much from fear. The question was his secret. What is certain is what is most questionable. Because he understood so much, he could not know anything. It was his business to question whatever presented itself as knowledge. What is the anxiety concerning gain or loss to one who *believes* he knows nothing? For one who *really* knows nothing, the process of the world yields *only* gain and loss. It is not possible to decide which of the two is better. His inability to know virtue seems to have its most profound consequence with respect to manifestly evil acts; is not Satan even in his rebellion against heaven condemned to continue to do the work of the Lord?

Yes. Socrates knew nothing at all, and it was because he was manifestly familiar with things and how they happened. He had an understanding of the world in abundance. Socrates' so-called skepticism was not so radical as to stifle all action. Doubt is, after all, transparent to *belief*. Understanding is not so much what is known as what is demonstrated in activity. To understand something in the sense I am using the term here does not mean to know something in the sense of having possession of some trans-temporal proposition. Rather to understand indicates a posture and an inclination to *stand under* or stand in obedience to how something goes. Understanding: a line of troops *stand* obediently *under* their commander. In German, *vorstanden* these troops *stand before* their commander. Real understanding obtains in toiling with the familiar. In living, I become familiar with my environment. My environment is that to which I may be subject or with which I may unify. So when I really understand, there is no doubt, and so to say that I am obedient to my understanding, is to be descriptive and not proscriptive. I am obedient to how it goes for me, and not to my idea about how it should go.

But the transparency of doubt is a flickering thing. Knowledge, in its desire to master that over which it presides, moves away uncertainty by denying change and so moving in a direction different from that of familiarity. Familiarity is, and so is manifest in my obedience to the process of the world, which it understands. Understanding is not the subject of epistemology and knowledge in its efforts to transcend change is always skeptical.

When Socrates said that he did not know, he meant that he was unable to confirm his most trusted beliefs. He was unable to confirm the relationship between his ideas about the world and his experience of that same world. It is between ideation and engaged experience that wonder takes its nourishment. To believe and not to know is to wonder.

Before the transcendental was posited (perhaps this was a time that never was), nothing was known. There was no problem of knowledge but only understanding and its obedience. When Plato's Socrates conceived the possibility that the idea of a particular entity, its eidos – the look of it – might be the fixed point of reality in a cosmos manifestly and disturbingly in flux, a new problem appeared: the problem of knowledge. Entities were given by the idea of them. Ideas, which are seemingly not in time, cannot be directly experienced, they cannot even be mine, and so it was not clear how the Forms of the sensible entities could be known. Plato told such stories and epistemology was born.

Because Plato's dialogues are so disrupted by irony, I am unable to discern the strength of Socrates' grip upon belief: how tightly or how loosely he held to his beliefs. Moreover, I cannot tell if this failing of mine is a problem in Plato or with me? Does Platonic irony obtain for me, in place of questions because I have always *known* too much? I have too compiled a list of those things whose loss *I know* I could not endure or whose possession *I know* is beyond my reach? To be afraid requires that I *know* what is to come, and that I *believe*, more or less, in what I know. To understand is to lean forward without fear. It is to manifest human temporality in its wholeness, ignoring the shards of its ideation: the past, the present and the future.

2.12

Not only does grief seem to have fingers too thick to unknot the tangle of my relations to the past, but also the oceanic sense of nostalgic grief that sometimes overwhelms me feels a little bit *too good* to be true. Such bittersweet longings seem as promiscuous as the aesthetic experience. I read a novel and, still weeping, pick up another. Nostalgia can be felt as a kind of grief: a pain for home and a time that is no more, a longing for an impossible return, a longing that properly belongs to defeat. But am I able actually to experience the impossibility of return when I am awash in longing for what I seem to think is impossible? Is defeat ever possible when I am caught in the grip of the nostalgic as strong and as blind as Polyphemus upon the mountains of his home raging at *no one* for punishing his one-eyed lack of hospitality?

It seems beyond doubt that the reasons I hunt are shot through with nostalgia. But nostalgia was not what began my consideration of hunting. I did not begin to consider or describe my relationship to my grandfather because I felt nostalgic for him. The mood that first caught my attention was almost the opposite of nostalgic longing. What began my thoughts about hunting and the quality of my relations to the past was finding myself caught up in an odd and uncanny repetition. I emerged from my involvement with oranges and knives in the kitchen in San Pedro and quite innocently found myself enacting a distant but familiar memory of a grandfather. I remembered him by being him. What was both familiar and strange about the incident was that I found him to be who I was, and the past went right on changing under my feet.

Three

3.0

June 1971. Trying to maintain an apartment downtown with my first wife, I took a job in the carpentry section of a maintenance company that took care of 102 funeral parlors in Manhattan. I was nineteen. Prior to this work, I had never seen a dead human body. Within weeks, I had seen hundreds. Naked, under sheets, sporting toe-tags tied over long untrimmed nails, the cadavers were lined up in the basement halls on gurneys: name, sex and age. The morticians rolled them in and out of the embalming rooms. I once touched the face of an old man. What I remember most about my mother's death was the coldness of her brow. Lying in bed, with the sheet pulled to her chin, it seemed she might be sleeping. When my hand touched her forehead and all doubt vanished.

The dead in the funeral parlors were mostly older persons, their corpses more weird than frightening. The oscillation between horror and attraction slowed after a week or so, and the tone of being around so many cadavers dropped an octave. I grew accustomed to their presence. Corpses are unlike other entities. There once human quality is loud. And then quite out of nowhere, the thought of finding a young person, dead and cold, flashed in my head at some point during the summer. The idea took hold and grew both appalling and irresistible. I looked without looking. Then the thought of finding a young woman dead and naked, maybe even beautiful, under a sheet in the darkness of the basement occurred to me. I was as horrified as you probably are now and did not allow myself to think about it.

Achilleus takes Briseis into his shelter and into his bed. A prize of war, she is also a beautiful young woman in a camp of foreign and dangerous men. She is in shock. All she had known is destroyed. The smells of her city – sacked and burned – are still fresh in her nostrils. She is unable to resist Achilleus any more than her city was able to stand against him. Neither can she forbear her desire to have a place. And so finally she cannot ignore the excitement of penetration and the relief that comes with the intromission of intimacy in a world at war I can barely imagine.

Achilleus tells Agamemnon that he loves the girl. Does this make sense? Perhaps Achilleus' wrath, born from the bitter aggravation of being cheated by Agamemnon, was actually nurtured more by the loss of the girl Briseis than it was fed by the loss of his prize, a mere token of honor, the value of which he had begun to question? Young men become very attached to young women, even if their attachment is most acutely felt in separation or threat of loss.

Opened by longing, Achilleus quickly loses track of the fact that the explicit flowering of his attraction for the girl has its root sunk into the lightless ground of the arbitrary. Why should she see any better? The quiddity of friendship is something political – possible only between equals – but love, erotic desire and the relations that belong to the domestic and the private, demands no such parity. Erotic desire *makes* us equal. Achilleus commands the love of the girl and perhaps is commanded by this love in return. A weaker man may seek to have such power over only the dead.

Traitors against the English crown in the sixteenth century were often hanged, drawn and quartered in front of cheering and jeering crowds. I remember as a schoolboy reading detailed accounts of the hangman's part in the grisly evisceration of the traitor. I was filled with a combination of fascination and repulsion so powerful that I was only able to read a sentence or two before I would feel compelled to cover the page with my hands. But after a moment, I was equally compelled to look down at the book and continue reading. As with Leontius outside the gates of Athens, who could not keep himself from looking at the carnage of a criminal butchered by the city's executioner, my appetite for the spectacle of death and dead bodies is as bipolar as the status of killing itself. The fact that slaughter is as attractive as it is repulsive puts me face to face with the fact that killing is not only sometimes necessary, it can be pleasurable as well. The quality of pleasure taken in violence may be related to revenge and the pleasures of justified anger or the pleasure may spill over into the demonic. It is impossible not to understand that great pleasure has been taken in slaughter of the weak and the helpless, even if we refuse to know it or hide our eyes from this horrible fact.

Our tradition has preserved accounts of the kinds of relations that sometimes obtain between erotic pleasure and violence: bacchanal bloodlust and various orgiastic rites blending orgasm and blood, sometimes – in fact, most times – the blood of the innocent and the powerless. But in every case, violence, once loosed, seems mostly to seek out the available. To take pleasure in doing violence to the merely available smacks of decadence. That hunting can be decadent is beyond doubt.

3.1

Ortega y Gasset's essay, *Meditations on Hunting*, was first written as a substantive introduction to a long and edifying treatise on sport hunting. The treatise, written by a Spanish nobleman, contends with various kinds of game, their habits and methods of capture, but it is also well-stocked with anecdotal stories concerning aristocratic hunters, guides and the quest for exotic game in the wilds of distant continents. Ortega y Gasset's introduction was published separately several years later. In it, he has a tendency to keep hunting situated within the context of the aristocratic. He both assumes and demonstrates the noble nature of hunting and does so in two registers: hunting as an activity favored by the social aristocracy and as an activity appropriate to a natural aristocracy.

Hunting has long been a symbol of social privilege. The English yeoman, on the eve of North American colonization, took umbrage with the local clergy for a multitude of reasons, not the least of which was the cleric's fondness of the field. The parish priest, often a pluralist, was all too often found coursing hare with the local gentry while a barely literate curate was left to tend the flock. Tolstoy writes that in Russia during the Napoleonic period a good wolfhound had a value exceeding that of a serf, and, in certain exceptional cases, a value that exceeded the worth of a whole village. Over hundreds, perhaps thousands of years, the right to hunt in Europe has almost entirely accreted to the landed classes.

Sport was a privilege desired by more than had it. After the French revolution, one of the first acts of the liberated middle class was to fish the streams of the countryside, previously a rigorously protected prerogative of the landed classes. Despite the jealousy with which great families guarded their hunting and fishing rights, the ruling classes were never completely successful in keeping the poor from the chase. In Europe, poaching and sport hunting are parallel traditions. Sometimes the local population was sufficiently isolated from baronial control that hunting could be done without much consequence. At other times, even under the nose of a very powerful landholder and at great risk of punishment, some men were still inclined to poach. Hunting and entitlement, even freedom, are persistently linked in the European sensibility. In the New World, in the English Colonies, the right to hunt was more or less universal. Even on private property, permission to hunt was easily given to the person who asked. Only recently has the relationship between hunting and property been asserted as broadly as we find it today in the United States.

An early seventeenth century account of the approach to the North American continent speaks about the scent of wild flowers while still two hundred miles at sea. New York harbor was a churning shoal. Salmon, bass and shad ran thick and hard. The meadowlands – where now a sports stadium and a shopping mall stand on the wreckage and waste of the industrial revolution – was nursery to the Atlantic and home to millions of migratory birds. Off Staten Island, there were oysters a half a foot across, geese and ducks in unimaginable numbers, muskrat, deer, fox: the mass of life was as astounding as its diversity. In the New World, hunting became economically important in ways that had been subducted under the development of the European continent and its culture hundreds of years before.

Game made up a meaningful part of the colonial diet, while deerskins from South Carolina and furs from the north provided the hard currency colonists needed to buy the imported manufactured goods they needed. Even if the majority of the skins and furs were supplied through barter that ultimately depended on the skills of native hunters, some of the early settlers became accomplished professional hunters and served both the local urban needs of town and city persons, as well as those of more distant European markets. Later, folk heroes Daniel Boone, Davy Crockett, and even Buffalo Bill – wilderness hunters and explorers – became cultural icons reflecting, perhaps even forming, cherished national values: courage, independence, toughness, resourcefulness and a certain, if perhaps dark, relationship to nature. My own grandfather was said to have hunted alligators in Louisiana to raise some cash on his way west at the very end of the nineteenth century. The frontier-hunter was admired and his skills praised. He was widely understood to be something of a natural aristocrat.

The word aristocracy is a Greek compound meaning something like power in the hands of the virtuous or the best. *Aristos*, particularly in Plato, has a meaning that is sometimes coupled to a notion of fundamental nature. The best horse is the horse in which the quiddity of horse – speed, strength, spirit, beauty, et cetera – was most manifest. This quiddity was the aristos of horse-ness. Conforming to the sense in which gold is said to be true, 'aristos' was later translated into Latin as a word related to the word for 'truth,' a word that is also related to the English word 'virtue.' In ancient philosophical texts, virtue is a common English translation of the word aristos. Both Plato and Aristotle used the term 'aristocracy' in their discussions of political science, but in a sense that was closer to our sense of a meritocracy than the kind of hereditary plutocracy by which we have come to understand the term. What is aristocratic in a natural sense is that which is inherently noble or best. Ultimately, the natural aristocrat is that person who most fully manifests human being or what a human being is.

Despite a history of approbation sometimes approaching veneration, the American hunter is no longer valued as widely or as much as he once was. I am not suggesting he should be: the world changes. But as a result of the dubious ethical status of hunting and hunters we find today, any nod towards the nobility of the sport has become a gesture of questionable taste. As ever-mounting social forces oppose hunting, participation in the sport has not been seen as an activity that promotes self-reliance or tests one's character so as much as a sadistic and barbaric display of aggression towards the natural environment – a display, some say, that should no longer be tolerated by a civilized people.

As with everything else that gains its authority from the past, hunting and killing of animals does not have any obvious ethical sanction. Voices from the past, the tradition, have opportunely broken through an effected independence, made suggestions, offered hope and even admonished when I have been without bearings of my own. But I have discovered that these ghosts to whom I have sometimes appealed will not speak without a sip of blood. The tradition says nothing of value without first tasting the flesh of my own understanding. Without offering myself to the dead, the tradition is merely a collection of artifacts – written and plastic articles dropped along the path of disembodied human development. These relics tell a story concerning one I no longer am. The multitude of its voices is the babbling, no matter how pleasant, of a fomenting past.

So while making an effort to uncover a sense in which hunting may participate in a natural *aristos* or virtue, I need to be as careful as I can possibly be not to celebrate any mindless killing or violence merely for the sake of unification. Without committing to any claim that is too large about the relation of hunting to virtue, or even beginning to refute the charge that hunting is *also* decadent, I would like to return to Ortega y Gasset and sort through some of what he has said about hunting and its relationship to human excellence, and in particular work through what amounts to an astonishing claim for nostalgia.

3.2

With the advent of modern technology, a foundational crisis undermining mathematics and nagging the sciences, the death of God, and perhaps even the end of experience, a systemic nostalgia seems to infuse the substrate of early twentieth century European thought. Ortega y Gasset, in step with many thinkers of his time, looks back to better days when the expression and fulfillment of our most base desires was possible. But we have evolved. Contemporary persons hunt within a long shadow cast before our progress, a progress Ortega y Gasset strongly connects to the atrophy of fundamental organic drives. The urge to chase and to kill has weakened, but not disappeared. The satisfaction of certain vestigial instincts turns out to be not only enjoyable, but a way back to something like origin. Origin appears in its enactment. It is because the pleasures one takes from such original modes of being are not just physical but also existential that hunting gets said to be a pastime appropriate to the natural aristocrat.

I startle at the sound of a window crashing down in the next room. Reflex. Instinct is the cause of an action over which the agent has little choice – what one does naturally. Breathing. But for Ortega y Gasset choice is the issue. *Who I am* results from the choices I make: what I have done, what I have not done. But I cannot be whatever I want to be. Common usage has already stipulated that who I am is subject and never object to my own constructive will. I may breathe or not breathe but I cannot hold my breath forever. Already I am my choices and have found myself in a world that does not always bend to my will. Choice is subject to disappointment. And so self-creation, perhaps like every other duty, is sometimes a burden.

While readily acknowledging that hunting can, and even should, meet some of our material needs, Ortega y Gasset maintains that the modern hunter takes to the field mostly for the sake of satisfying a mode of nostalgia that stems from the very nature of human existence. In leaning towards the gratification of my more original urges, hunting frees me from the existential responsibility that necessarily falls to one who becomes through choice. Such is the case (even if this freedom is only tasted) because he has noticed that hunting shares in the same kind of temporality associated with the *best* vacation spots: the timelessness of a mountainscape, the unhurried pace of a tropical island. To hunt, the Spanish philosopher writes, is to "vacation in the Paleolithic."

This bizarre locution seems to articulate the center of Ortega y Gasset's *A Meditation on Hunting*. But it would be a mistake to think the pronouncement embraces science fiction. He is not interested in traveling through time. He is interested in a way to be that turns out to be trans-temporal. Hunting designates a mode of being that transgresses and so erases the usual differences between past, future and present. To "vacation in the Paleolithic" is to collapse time.

When I hunt, I am taken over by a more ancient temporality. *Now* I follow the track of the elk that was here an hour ago so that I might kill it in the meadow later this afternoon. Time is unified in the single act expressed by the preceding sentence. *Who I am* vanishes into the temporal thickness of the hunt that does not separate the future from the past. Like a flickering lamp, I push into the darkness of the quest and, in having vanished into the wild, in *being at home* in the wild, in being complete, I put down the existential burden of self-creation. Nostalgic longing is sated because I am absorbed into a way to be that will not support the temporal modes by which self-creation is made possible. Not every kind of nostalgic longing is a whimsical dreaming into a perfect past – a past that has already been sealed away from experience. Nostalgia may also be the longing for the taste of existential freedom, the thirst to be at home everywhere. This kind of nostalgia is quenched in the chase.

Even if hunting is actually able to satisfy the longing for existential freedom by direct experiential access to that for which this kind of nostalgia longs – a kind of absorption into, and so being at home in the wild – there are several issues pertaining to the aristocratic nature of the quest that remain clouded. It is not clear whether the more original state of being that I am suggesting is achieved in hunting is the best way for human being to be. Or, if hunting is a mode of access to some way to be that is the best or most authentic, it is not obvious that hunting is the best way to develop this way to be.

3.3

Hunting is never a harmless walk in the woods. In killing anything, for most any reason, a person cannot quite say he has done a good thing. Yet nearly every culture, and so nearly every person, seems to claim that under the right circumstances killing is permitted: for food, in self-defense, as punishment, to preserve the ones we love or the nation. In an ever-expanding sense, survival is taken to be a natural right and is almost never actually subordinated to equally ubiquitous prohibitions against killing. When killing is sanctioned in some sense or other, it is often wrapped in ritual, odd customs and mysterious codes. In the space between a killing and its justification opens a field of many and motley acts of propitiation, obviation and obfuscation. At the very least, anxiety pervades the act of killing. The acts of ceremony, conciliation and reconciliation that are a matter of custom demonstrate publicly some of the disquiet that belongs to the taking of a life – acts that generally seem to smooth the way towards a kind of forgetting of the dead. The subsistence hunter often pays homage to the animals he kills.

Eskimos are inclined to speak to the animal or its spirit-guardian after a kill. The hunter might beg for pardon and otherwise adopt a conciliatory manner toward the animal's soul and the spirit or god that protects it. Native hunters do not seem to blanch at bald lies. It is as if they are trying to convince the spirit world that the death of the animal was an aberration. The point of the hunter's apostrophe seems to be to situate the animal's death within a blameless setting: I am so sorry to have killed you; it was an accident. My arrow flew off the string. You understand. We need your flesh. I'm sure you will not mind. My children are hungry...

The traditional subsistence hunter makes his atonement not because of any psychological guilt he might have about killing the animal, but because he is afraid that an unpropitiated spirit will queer future hunts. The hunter propitiates the dead out of respect not just for the animal that has died but also for the greater cycle of life and death: the spirit or god that cares for both the living and the dead. Out of respect, the killing must be acknowledged or cleansed. Purification sometimes is a kind of magic performed to lull to sleep the protecting spirits of the animal world. Elaborate expiations for successful hunts occur in indigenous cultures that unambiguously permit and utterly depend upon the killing of animals. The traditional hunter appeases the souls of the animals he kills without respect to the fact that he plans to continue to kill.

The thought that hunting might be an ethical problem never crosses the mind of the hunter when he is fully engaged in the hunt. Once the animal lies dead, the modern hunter perhaps has a tinge of guilt as the Paleolithic recedes leaving a corpse at his feet – at least until he gets to work preparing the carcass. The modern hunter pays his respects in his obedience to certain codes: a clean kill and using as much of the animal as possible. Each is involved in something like a ceremony. These acts of conciliation move to liquidate blame. The modern hunter, the indigenous hunter, each asserts the practicality of his act. The indigenous hunter tries to curry favor by pointing to necessity as the ultimate cause of the animal's misfortune: It was not my fault. I had to do it. The hunter asks that his deeds be forgotten, not because he is sorry that he has killed but because he has acted out of necessity. It is as if in pleading necessity the hunter announces his connection to and his place in the natural world. Of course, the spirit world does not seem as actual to me as perhaps it does to the traditional hunter-gatherer. I am also a creature of my time. Spirits seem like the superstitions of others to me. It is unclear how much I should differentiate primitive pieties from my own obedience to and concerns for ethical principle.

Four

4.0

Like Gregor Samsa, the gored horse struggled with its hooves in the air that it might win its feet again. I have no memory of the aficionados who must have been rushing to get out of the way. In a single heave of the bull's neck, man, lance and the ancient, well-padded horse were lifted from the ground and pitched into the second row of the stadium. Once the picador had been disposed of, the bull turned to make everything else that confronted him disappear. Thirty-five years ago I was eighteen years old, fresh out of high school and living alone in a strange Spanish city. I had never seen such a thing in my life.

It was a good fight. The tail or the ears or both were awarded. Dead, his hind legs were lashed to a spar, which was in turn harnessed to a team of horses. Black and bloody, the bull was dragged around the ring in a blizzard of flowers and cheers before being pulled into a tunnel that led beneath the bleachers in which I was sitting. It was over. Taken by an impulse to follow, I left my seat, while others were still clapping and yelling. I moved quickly to the exit. Looking for a way to the base of the stadium, I found a set of stairs and within a few minutes discovered a large chamber formed by the massive arches supporting the bullring in Barcelona.

The dead bull was already there. He had been drawn down the tunnel and onto a smooth floor of fitted stone. Freed from the harness and the team, the spar, to which the bull was tied, was being made up to a set of blocks that hung from the overhead. The horses had been led off to the side and were tethered to an iron ring set in one of the gray stone columns. All around the bull, men in leather aprons worked with knives. Two or three others had already started to cinch up on the blocks. As the spar came away from the floor, the hide, on which the bright blood had been so dramatic, was peeled loose and soon lay heaped on the stones under a steaming side of beef. The body of the hunted animal is also put to use, but neither is the hunt merely the production of meat.

4.1

In hunting the real work, it is said, does not begin until after you pull the trigger. The guests at the mountain ranch liked to see the llamas about the place, as they also liked the lanky Texas 'long horns' kept in the big pasture close to the cabins. Their preferences together with the fact that Las Cruces is hot and dry in summer caused Stuart to come to an arrangement. He would load his herd onto a long-low stock trailer in the spring and haul them from his farm along the Rio Grande to a guest ranch in Colorado just outside of Creed. It took a while. In the fall, he would drive back up to Creed and take the llamas south again. The round trip saved him from needing to feed the beasts for the summer. It was not unusual that one or more of Stuart's friends would accompany him on these drives, not only for the adventure but because in exchange for bringing his llamas to the ranch, Stuart and his entourage were given the run of the place for a few days. The fishing was outstanding: cold water and wild trout. My brother made the trip a couple of times.

Over the years I have heard a great deal about Bud. He lived on the ranch and was a guide. He was born in the same valley in which the main part of the ranch lay. His people were small ranchers and, like everyone else up there, made ends meet doing a little bit of everything. I have been told he left the state just once and that was to fight in the Second World War. As a boy, Bud hunted elk with a rifle. Later, he used a re-curve bow. When he was in his sixties, he took pleasure in sneaking up on elk browsing in the snow and giving them a slap on their brown haunches – a story as credible as the one Theodore Roosevelt tells about a mountain man who could jump out of a barrel without touching the sides and was reputed to have killed grizzly bears in a most unorthodox manner. His dogs would track and then hold the bear at bay. While the bear was distracted by the dogs, the hunter would slip around behind it, push a long serpentine knife through the bear's back ribs in just the right spot and hollow out the heart with a violent twisting motion.

I understand that Bud, like other ranchers I've met, was a reticent man and disinclined to tell hunting stories. But there was an exception. His boy made a trip to bow hunt in the vast boglands for which this southern part of moose-rich Alaska is famous. The moose can be huge and Bud's son was alone. After having stalked and killed a bull, he found he had gotten himself ten miles from the nearest trailhead. It took four trips to pack out the bull. The meat was sweet and the rack is on the barn. That was the story Bud told.

I am sure it was an effort for Bud's son to find a bull. Moose hunting in that part of the state is very physical and bow hunting is always a challenge, but that was not the point. In his mid-thirties at the time, his son would have had to pack out the meat and the rack by himself. The walk could not have been less than eighty miles as the crow flies, but half that distance would have been covered carrying some very serious weight. The moose was unlikely to have weighed less than nine hundred pounds and could have come in at twice that. Even if all the meat were boned and bagged, a chore in itself, even if one were not inclined, as one should be by the letter of the law, to get every last piece from the carcass, the weight Bud's son must have carried on his back through a bog in hip waders would have been staggering. Four trips were both too many and not enough.

With the death of the beast comes a shift in the nature of the hunt. The difficulties entailed in maintaining concentration and containing the passions of the hunt climax with the kill. The epoch of the questing experience wanes into the toils of the butcher and the bearer. Like becoming a father, through which the complications of an erotic relationship transmogrify into the rearing and support of children, the woodcraft of the hunter gives over to labors made with economic ends in mind.

4.2

About two years ago, I was hunting quail in the desert west of Las Cruces, out alone with my dogs bouncing along a two-track. I saw a kit fox asleep in the road ahead of me and assumed the fox would wake and get out of my way. But I never saw it move. Without much thought, I glanced into the rear view mirror as I passed by. In the mirror, I saw the fox staggering like a drunk propped up against a jam and wondered if I had run over it. I quickly dismissed the idea as impossible in much the same way I dismissed the bewildered look I had imagined on the face of the fox. But on my way back to the main road, for I had not forgotten, I saw the fox dead on the side of the two-track just about where I had seen him in the rear view mirror. Had I been hunting for fox, I would have been pleased to kill him. But I had not been hunting fox and I went back to town without stopping and hauntingly ashamed, haunted by something about clumsiness or catastrophe.

The kill disconnects the quarry from its body. The animal hunted, like the last breath of a man, vanishes into the mystery from which it came. In its place are packages of meat. In death, the animal becomes something other than a corpse over which I mourn. It becomes something I use – without use perhaps I would always grieve? I nourish myself with its meat, not dead animal muscle. When I eat the flesh of an animal, the living animal has not only been eclipsed but also transformed. I do not eat a pig or a cow. I eat pork or beef. The labor of preparing game for the table trails in its wake both a conversion and a forgetting.

There is a scene in a contemporary Mexican film in which quail are prepared with a rose sauce made from a bouquet given a young girl by her forbidden lover. The girl is cook and magician. Her guests salivate over the birds crisped in a broiler. What the guests have most in common with these animals – the urge to live – has been distilled into an essence, into a fragrance and a taste. The dish turns out to be an aphrodisiac of remarkable potency that disrupts the household in an altogether funny, appropriate and touching manner. In this comedy, the transformation from animal to meat is delicious and hopeful. In the tragedy, the meal prepared by the lover and mother is sometimes the horror of a bitter flood that drowns the bloodline of a father who consumes the flesh of his own children prepared in a stew. The mysteries of flesh know no bounds.

Even if I usually eat meat and not flesh, it is still possible to encounter flesh as having been alive. Conscious or explicit involvement in and with the flesh of the dead is not usual. What I mean is that meat-eaters, doctors, butchers, cooks and morticians have for the most part lost contact with the particular body before them as having been alive – though they know perfectly well that the hamburger in my hand, the cadaver on which the doctor is performing an autopsy or the crown roast the cook is basting was once a living creature. When I have explicitly encountered flesh as the muscle of a once living animal, I have usually moved quickly through a sense of strangeness and become disgusted or entered into the realm of the orgiastic. The quirky horror of meat on the tongue, real or imagined, is part of almost everyone's experience. In some persons this sense is strong and in others weak. Orgiastic abandon may be hard to locate in one's personal experience, but it haunts literature and myth: the pre-patriarchal blood feasts in a time so dark there is only a flicker of this fire left in the civilized world. Perhaps we catch a glimpse of this fascination with flesh in *The Bacchantes* or even in the fire that burns in Plato's cave. Perhaps the same poetic magic that, mocking the sun, made shadow appear in that cave also rendered the aphrodisiac from the quail in its rose sauce – a magic that makes either disgust or pleasure. Killing animals and eating their bodies is the everyday all mixed up with the mystical in ways obvious and obscure.

4.3

Peter Freuchen made several expeditions into the deep north and then unexpectedly vanished. The Danish explorer, as it turns out, spent ten years with an Inuit wife living in Greenland in summer and on the ice cap in winter and only returned to civilization after she died. He never wrote about his time with her except to say that it had been the best ten years of his life. In the artic, all there is to eat is meat.

At the end of the summer when most of the arctic creatures start south, the polar Eskimo waits for the pack ice to freeze solid and moves north to winter along with the polar bear. In this environment, both man and bear live mostly on seals. The material existence of the so-called polar Eskimo was an extraordinarily thin affair and perhaps it is a consequence of their material fragility that the Inuit peoples of the far north seem to live with a vitality and in an immediacy with the world that I and many others have found compelling – at least within the compass of books and stories.

Up until the mid-twentieth century, the circumpolar Eskimo family groups relied exclusively on stone-age technology because until very recently the indigenous equipment was really the only gear able to meet the extremes in temperature and weather that characterize the far north. European explorers of the late nineteenth and early twentieth century who did not employ Inuit clothing and methods suffered and died. An account of expeditions to the North Pole prior to Byrd's provides a number of tragic examples of what happened to staunch men who preferred woolen coats and good English leather boots. Later explorers all wore native gear. But quite recently the hunters who go into this frozen country after musk ox, walrus and polar bear are encouraged to wear modern clothing. The native guides recommend the latest equipment to their clients and use it themselves: snowmobiles, exotic synthetic fabrics, wicking underwear and down. The migration of the men onto the ice cap in winter has all but vanished. It is conceivable that there were functioning stone age Eskimos as late as 1950 or 1960, but in all probability that culture disappeared sometime before the 1940s. The polar Eskimo, whose survival was completely dependent upon his enormous skill at finding and killing animals, might be taken as the paradigm of a people who must hunt for purely practical reasons. But such a conclusion is just as easily turned on its head. The existence of a culture as extreme as that of the polar Eskimo does not prove that man must hunt to live but that not even the polar ice in mid-winter is a deterrent to a people in quest of game.

Only a fool asks why we did not remain in the garden where all our needs ripened on the bough of a tree. There must have been lots of practical reasons to migrate: overpopulation, feud, war, scarcity of resources. Moving became necessary. The nature of this necessity found its way into myth. Man was expelled from paradise and born into the world as a result of his gaining knowledge of death. Perhaps at the same moment we gained knowledge of hunting as well?

4.4

A meat hunter is distinguished from one who hunts for horns. Big game hunting is a lot of trouble and has a way of getting expensive. Stuart says he is a meat hunter. Having grown up killing varmint with a twenty-two, hunting rabbit, deer, elk and quail, he only occasionally hunts big game anymore. He never did much trophy hunting. Still he likes to shoot some bunny, even if he is a little nervous about the plague these creatures carry. Killing big animals bothers him just enough that he is never quite enthusiastic about it anymore. If Stuart has lost some of his enthusiasm for hunting, it would be inaccurate to say he is squeamish about killing – when the right opportunity presents itself he kills without qualm. Nor would it be right to say that the thrill of the hunt does not affect him. These days, Stuart hunts birds in the desert. He hunts with me when I am around and I am grateful for his company. He has been a good friend for many years and generously taught me about hunting quail in the great southwest.

Some hunters claim to hunt for purely economic reasons. I don't. Others argue wild meat tastes better than domestic. I cannot say. For others, game meat is taken to be healthier than domestic animals grown for the purpose of slaughter. I have not thought much about it. Domestic meat is accused of being too processed: too artificial, too filled with drugs, too much fat. There are even ethical reasons given by some hunters for killing the meat you eat – at least for those who eat meat. Basically, the claim is really two. Meat is not (or should not be) a consumer good like other goods. Second, a hunter is more in touch with what it means to eat meat than a person who goes to the grocery store and buys a package of chops. When I was young, I certainly felt that if I ate meat it was better that I kill the animal myself than foist the task onto someone else. It seemed more ethical to do one's own dirty work. I am not as convinced of this point of view now. If killing animals is an ethical problem, how did I imagine I would escape responsibility by killing them myself? It may be more honorable to kill your own food, enemies, et cetera, but it is not more ethical.

Hunters for the Hungry is a not-for-profit group that distributes wild meat to the poor. If I look past the organization's good intentions, its existence is probably the best example I might use against the claim that hunting is merely a practical affair. Despite the uses that are made of the hunted animal's body, the idea that we kill merely for the sake of our own material needs ignores several facts, not the least of which is that modern hunting is, in most cases, very hard to account for by an analysis of its return on investment. It even seems likely to me that the possibility that we hunt for meat has always taken a share in the impractical. I realize the second claim might be controversial, but the first is not. We can all agree that in this era, at least abstractly or in most cases, there are more practical ways to feed and clothe oneself than hunting. The direct cost of hunting, for most hunters, is so high it is an embarrassment to discuss. The indirect cost of the wilderness is also getting higher all the time. Wild animal habitat has become a commodity like any other, and it does not make economic sense to set aside land for the sole purpose of providing a food source for hunters. Hunters for the Hungry attests to the fact the meat comes along after the hunt, almost as if by accident. You kill game and then you figure out what to do with it.

The indigenous peoples in North America who are trying to preserve what is left of their cultures assert their right to kill the animals of their regions not on practical grounds, as if they believe their material needs can only be met through hunting and fishing, but for cultural reasons. These identified ethnic groups wish to fish and hunt in order to maintain or even revive a way of life. There are cultural, and perhaps existential values belonging to the hunt that, even in a hunter-gatherer culture, outweigh hunting's raw practicality. Such reasons for hunting are not isolated to the indigenous hunter either. It is to social values that many modern American hunters appeal when called upon to defend their sport. Hunting, the argument goes, builds strong and good relationships inside families and communities – hunting is a bonding experience. Of course so is going to war.

4.5

Adopting the title 'meat hunter' makes primary one of the basic codes of hunting: one must eat (or put to use) what one kills. Just because hunting does not necessarily find its origin in the merely practical considerations of biological need, does not discount the fact that hunting is *also* practical. Practicality is an essential element of what is meant by hunting, which means that I must have some use for what is killed in order to be said to be hunting. Even varmint hunting is obedient to the principle of use. Animals are classified as varmints because they destroy property. Killing the varmint is practical in that it protects property. It seems that killing is always searching around for a justification. The connection between killing something and sustaining oneself is actually felt, but it is felt in the negative as a disconnect. One hunts for food but one does not hunt *merely* for food.

I remember a guide I once had saying that he was going to lodge a complaint with Fish and Game that some young and physically fit hunters had the habit of killing big elk up on the ridges and then packing out only the trophies and the choice cuts of meat. In every state in which I have hunted, it has always been a criminal offense to leave in the field any part of a game animal killed that is consumable by a human.

In 1936, my father and both his parents were driving out somewhere near Spokane, Washington, in *the Pierce Arrow*, as my father used to say – an elegant, half open car with a great huge hood and fine flat grill. As they came around a turn, a buzzard found itself unable to build up sufficient speed to take off from the road. The car struck the scavenger and killed it against the grill. Much to the horror of my grandmother, my granddad stopped the car and pulled to the side of the road saying or perhaps muttering: "if you kill it you eat it." He was wearing a coat and tie. He took off his coat, rolled up his sleeves, plucked and gutted the bird, built a fire and ate the thing while his wife and my father huddled together in the back seat of the car. As far as I know, a buzzard is not considered either a game animal or a varmint.

4.6

Of all the ways in which we kill animals, the rearing and slaughtering of domestic animals seems to be the most closely tied to the production of meat. A hunt is less exclusively tied to the practical. What constitutes a bullfight has even less to do with the *mere* production of meat than a hunting expedition. Death necessarily concludes both the hunt and the bullfight, but the act of killing defines neither. The bullfight and the hunt are alike in other ways as well.

There is a strange asymmetry between the intent of the bull and the intent of the matador. The bull in his rage strives to make those who have been placed in front of him go away, whereas the matador is neither angry nor trying to make the bull disappear. This asymmetry brings forward a quiddity belonging to the bullfight that is shared with the hunt. Quite contrary to the intent of the bull, the matador wishes to make the bull appear. Naturally, I do not mean that the matador aims at making the bull *merely* appear, but to appear in its virtue as a bull. Danger is essential to the bullfight and opens the space in which the bull is to demonstrate his own virtue. In the face of danger, the bullfighter summons that which makes a bull a *good* bull – what Aristotle would call the virtue of the bull – and it is precisely here that another feature shared by hunting and bullfighting manifest. The bullfighter and the hunter are both conjurers of animals. The bullfighter has the bull show up as brave. The hunter causes the animal to appear on the field in its availability to his weapons.

Unlike a hunt, the bullfight has some of the character of the theater. But bullfighting is a spectacle that only *half* engages the 'as if' that belongs to dramatic performance. Players enter the ring to the sound of a horn: two *picadors*, three *banderil-leros*, the *torero*. The bull is bred from an ancient race. The tendons of the bull's neck are weakened and cut with lances and sharpened barbs. The head and horns drop and expose the space between the shoulder blades under which beats the bull's heart. The blood runs. There is a final blast of the horn and the matador appears. He approaches the bull as if to fight, but then there is the *veronica*. The spectacle is not so much a fight as a dance – a dance done to rhythms of real and actual danger. The cape grows smaller, the dance more intense. A sword appears from the red folds of the *muleta* and the bull's heart is pierced or the aorta is cut. The character of the performance is suddenly revealed. The *Corrida* is neither combat nor theater, but a kind of piety. The virtue of the bull is first demonstrated and then given away or offered up. The bull's excellence shows in the dance between man and beast and is not disclosed in the bull's death or the matador's bravery. The former unmasks the matador as priest and the latter measures the matador's *faena* or mastery of the bull alone in the same way the cleanness of the kill is to the credit or disgrace of the hunter.

Five

5.0

In order to hunt something in the wild there must always be a reasonable chance of catching the game that is sought. I cannot hunt things that are not there. A tiger hunt along the Hudson River is not hunting. On the other hand, if I were to walk into a field of deer tame to the hand and shoot one down with a pistol, I should not say I had been hunting either. Hunting is not merely a way to kill an animal. I do not hunt chickens in a barnyard in much the same way I do not fish in a barrel. It has long been understood that game is scarce as a matter of principle. When I say that the Owyhee is covered up with chukar, in some modality, scarcity obtains along with these birds as part of what it means to speak of them as game. Hunting is foremost a quest.

Neither is hunting a competition. Against his quarry, even dangerous game – bear, lion, cape buffalo, et cetera – the hunter is *expected* to kill the beast. It is an accident if the hunter is injured or killed and it is always unfortunate if no game is found. The point is that game never 'wins,' even when it gets away. So even if hunting cannot be defined as successfully killing the quarry, the hunt comes to its proper conclusion only when game is killed. With respect to other hunters, if I hunt with friends and find that I am competitive with them, it is only to my shame. A full game bag is surely a good thing and something about which one should be grateful, but the hunt is at bottom tied to that which is given. In an important sense, being good at the hunting means being properly prepared to receive what is given. No matter how skillful the hunter, luck always plays a part. Developing hunting skills is a matter of respect for what is there more than a matter of personal accomplishment. To hunt is a way to be that has been handed down. It comes complete with its codes and practices. I do not determine what hunting is by my behavior. Who I am gets taken over in the hunt. In the most authentic moments of the chase, it might even be said that who I am is not even there.

Why must I kill what I hunt? Why not take a picture and eat a peanut butter sandwich? I am capable of asking such questions only when I think about hunting. When I am actually hunting, the bull elk does not show up as a wonder of nature. Rather the animal is encountered in its availability to my weapons. In hunting, the animal is game and is there to be killed. When I think about hunting my prey, making game gets broken into steps. One: find the bull. Two: stalk him. Three: take aim and shoot. Only after hunting has been sundered in a storm of thought do I discover that thinking, like "all the king's men," lacks the power to weld finding game and killing game back together again. That the whole is always greater than its parts is a mystery I cannot explain.

Of course, when I am not hunting but rather standing before the question of hunting, the reasons I hunt spring up like mushrooms along a grassy dyke: I hunt for meat; I hunt for the challenge; for fun; to be in nature; to bond with friends and family. Such assertions are true but, nevertheless, open more questions than they answer. They therefore function more efficiently in covering up the quiddity of the hunt than disclosing it. But I can still remember when hunting through the trees, my prey was there in the shadows of the timber. As a hunter who is hunting, I do not come across the bull elk and then decide to shoot it. In *making game*, the bull shows up in his availability to being killed. The hunter looks for elk with a rifle.

5.1

A good friend of mine was hunting elk in the Sawtooth Mountains of Idaho. Bob happened to have a mountain lion tag in his pocket. Idaho Fish and Game seems to sell state-resident big-game tags in a triptych: elk, mountain lion and bear. After a long morning working hard in the severe country, he sat down against the trunk of a large pine to take a midday rest. No sooner had he settled than a mountain lion walked out of the timber. The big cat looked at Bob, moved across the clearing between them, lay down under a tree not forty feet away and went to sleep. It is unusual to see a mountain lion in the wild. They are aloof, but it would be a mistake to suppose that these animals are fearful. These big cats seem rather to do pretty much as they please. Bob watched the lion for twenty minutes fully aware of the tag in his pocket and with a loaded rifle across his knee until the lion stood up, looked at him again and ambled back into the wild. Bob later told me he had barely thought about shooting the animal and he almost no desire to do so. It did not seem right. Without respect for the tag in his pocket, he was there to hunt elk, not mountain lion.

5.2

I was in Utah to hunt deer. I pulled off the fire road, stepped from the truck, loaded my rifle and clicked the safety on. I was thinking about where to go, if I had enough water and food with me and whether or not should I lock the truck. I wanted to get back to the cabin a couple of hours before dark so that I might get some work done. It was a half hour before dawn. I would hunt until lunch. As I started to move away from the truck, I slung my rifle on my left shoulder and simultaneously jumped up a legal buck. I had not taken ten steps from the door of my vehicle. Had I killed the little buck it would have been because I had managed to shoulder the rifle, click off the safety and swing the barrel around before the buck vanished down the slope. I would not have killed him because I was hunting. In fact, that buck was long gone before I even really thought about shooting him.

5.3

As long as I am actually hunting, I cannot suffer *buck fever*. I do not startle. I do not jerk the trigger and I do not miss. To be fully engaged in the quest is to lose the capacity for surprise or suffer a burst of nerves. In scouring the countryside for game, no one is there to imagine game. In losing oneself to searching, there is no one there to dream of the future. Who I am dissolves into making game. For me to get excited about killing an animal means I have projected a future in which the animal is to be killed. When I vanish, the past, the future, even the present vanish with me. There is only a purposeful leaning forward. Without a future, there can be no surprise.

The best shot, and perhaps the most successful hunter I know, once gave me some advice about buck fever. Not many years ago, he had gotten a little too excited about a bull elk standing at the far end of a meadow: a good sized, six-by-six herd bull. He began thinking how good the mount would look in his trophy room, about how pleased he would be to have his second success in the one season – he had already killed a cow – and proceeded to shoot over the elk's back at about two hundred yards. The bull was spared. Buck fever had struck my friend down. He looked at me and said with a determination I found somewhat unsettling that once he realized what had happened, he swore to himself right then that such a thing would never happen again. His lesson to me: daydreaming is cured only by an oath.

5.4

There is a saying about big game hunting that goes something like this: excitement for breakfast, desire for lunch and per-severance for dinner. The hunter who really wishes to hunt makes a pledge and then keeps it at every meal. My eye shall search absence and question shadow. My ears shall reach into the noiseless deep. Attention shall be kept in the wind. And I shall never let hope cover over the wild.

The hunter does not hope for game. He does not maintain himself towards his prey as if it were there. There is no fantasy. The activity of hunting is altogether different from imagining the animal where it is not. It is precisely the reverse. To make game, I imagine my prey to be exactly where it is.

Game is found by remaining alert, not by looking towards success or worrying about failure. One must hunt without a future. Do not think about the end of the day or the pleasures of the hearth and bed. When I am fully engaged by the activity of hunting the desire for game does not stimulate excitement for the kill but rather improves my endurance to be there. I vanish into a stand of ponderosa, the yellowing grass and the flitting of birds. I slip into the complicated currents that pass over the skin of my arm. Disappear into the scent of the soil and sink into earth as my shins press upon the soft ground. I have forgotten all the stories I know about myself. As I grow small, the world grows large.

It does not matter if I was hunting before or if I will be hunting again soon. I *make game* by opening to game in its being where and how it is. When absorbed into the hunt, there is no time for thought or dreams. The senses grow long. The difference between forest and sensation fades. Time thins. It vanishes like a mist. There is not even a present. Without past and future, there is no need for a present. There is only the steepness of the hill, the cold of the dawn.

I do not stay at home out of the weather. My desire to hunt is so strong I throw on a coat, lace up my boots and go into the wild. Walk for miles. Sit behind a tree. Walk again. Desire matters, but if I search for game through the optic of my excitement for success, I am going to catch buck fever – that excitement for a kill that interrupts the appearance of the animal as prey. Childish longing runs out ahead of my capacity to persist. Desire must mature. It must be plowed back into awareness. Difficulty becomes an ally. Physical exhaustion may be just enough to break down desire into the loam in which my attention roots. Concentration, counterintuitively, is made easier by the difficulty of the hunt. Up to a point, the harder the hunt the easier it is to hunt. When I tire, the edge of my enthusiasm dulls against the hardness of the trail and the future flows from my head into my feet. Not just me. The dogs hunt better a little tired as well. They run wild. Then they pant. They rest and settle into dogged effort. When I drop away, when I fold into the wild, my nervous eagerness for the kill soaks into the mountain soil and drains away into deep pools that reflect the sky and the interlacing of trees. Hunting depends on the fact that excitement may yet be transformed into perseverance as I vanish into the chase. I cannot know hunting at all.

5.5

The hunter in hunting is neither skeptical nor cynical. Skepticism and cynicism have to do with the kind of stance I might take towards a statement or a proposition. I take such stands all the time – I may be cynical about one thing and skeptical about another. But the hunter in allowing does not *know* where his prey is. He is open to game. There is no proposition against which the hunter can take a stand. Of course, the hunter has become familiar with his prey, its habits and its habitats. He understands. He may have a great deal of understanding, but it is his manifest ignorance that opens or may even be the space in which the animal manifests. Because he does not know where the deer is, the hunter extends to the margins of the forest where the trees give out into pasture. The desire for game is properly manifest in a specific kind of ignorance, a certain open space that is the occasion of game. Ignorance as a freedom from opinion or knowledge, is the basis for allowing the possible to manifest in accordance with its nature. Ignorance, understood as the being of a certain kind of absence, of a certain mindfulness, seems to be the basis of human creativity or making. It may also be the most proper expression of finitude, and complete embrace one can make of one's essential shame. For I cannot do one thing if I am doing another.

Finitude means *there could be more*. Availability is the essence of human finitude. To be creative is to be related to availability in accordance with what is available. To be in availability is to be aware. To be aware is to be without location, without context. Dreaming gives way to the keenness of an unfolding of what is about one as time collapses into wide-circumstance of availability. There is always more to availability than meets the eye. I can see only what is there in the offing. In allowing game to be *where it is* as *it is*, the hunter relates himself creatively to the givenness of game. There is no seeking. This is what it means to *make game*. The way of the hunter is to be the occasion for the appearance of game in its susceptibility to his weapons. Finite creation is an allowing. This kind of allowing is neither active nor passive but profoundly middle-voiced. The middle voice is not so much between the active and the passive as before. It is the most original form of action. Creativity allows what is sought to unfold in accordance with the particular nature of its contingency. Contingency is how I actually experience the abundance of what is given into the openness of the wild when making game.

The buck comes into view under the cedar in a way that may be compared to how a shotgun finds its form in the workshop. I am a gunsmith and so I have an explicit understanding of what a shotgun is and the procedures by which it comes to be. Familiar with the nature of the shotgun I am and its use. Its fit. Making a shotgun is possible for me. What is possible is rooted in the past. The materials have been sought and procured. I have enough experience to coax a barrel from hard billets of steel. I have taught my fingers to round the trigger with a file and paper, to tap threads into the nickel-rich casing. In making a shotgun, I enact a method which consists in practices that have been handed down to me. The act of gun making informs the modifications I make. In this way the gun finds its form in my allowing the materials to be worked as they should be worked: namely, in allowing particular parts and pieces to come together in accordance with the nature of a shotgun. I am a craftsman and so am capable of being fully engaged in the craft of gun making. There is no need to speak of allowing the gun to be as it should be. Craft articulates the gun as it *should be*. I keep the chisel sharp. The bench clean. The oil clear. In the most bizarre manner of speaking I can imagine, the gunsmith and the occasion of his craft, in his way to be is *the should* of how a gun is well made. There under the bench grows a pile of shaving from a blank of finely figured walnut. The gunsmith has vanished into his work and what does not belong to the gun drifts silently to the floor.

The creation of a shotgun, even including its proud new locking mechanism, is a manifestation of the past rooted in what is possible for a gun maker. Who knows where contingency is fastened? Who knows the past? A properly crafted shotgun – in manifesting the relationship between hunter and bird – is all that the past can ever be. The craftsman makes room for the gun on his bench as I make room for the deer under the sweet-smelling trees. The hunter does not lose track of the nature of his prey as something given, just as the craftsman does not lose track of the givenness of his creation within the order determined by the hunter's relationship to game.

At my bench and leather apron, I am no different from the gun stock I am checkering. In my disguises, costumes and camouflage, lying in the thickest parts of the bracken with rifle, knife and an open eye, I am no one at all. In the light of finite creation all pronouns have vanished like flames in the sunlight. Attentiveness not only makes possible the appearance of the thing made, but in the twinkling of the world, a pronoun may reemerge. As if by accident, 'I' may precipitate from the whole of the world-mist. I never appear because I am looking not for myself. When I first appear into uncanniness from my engagement with the world, my way to be is not so much a point of view as being everywhere at once. Perhaps I would be omniscient if I were not also blind. The sensation that accompanies the emergence of the self into the activity of the day is the strangeness that belongs to the sensation of again being the same: the uncanny, the mood of the familiar and the strange. My mood is experienced in a seamless manner with the world in which I am immersed. Such moments seem to have no practical weight whatsoever, and yet are set deep in memory. I am telling a story.

Six

6.0

My initiation to hunting was probably irregular. It may even have been corrupt. Even if it turns out the reasons I hunt are ultimately rooted in habits that belong to the most practical aspects of living, in a fundamental participation with 'the cycle of life,' and so to the 'cycle of death' to which every creature belongs and to which every human creature is subject, I have also found that my motives for hunting have sounded various levels of nostalgia: for a grandfather I loved and mourned; for a place and a time in which there was a better way to live. It may be the case that hunting has been a genuine if somewhat confused effort to be at home in a world that has so often showed up to me as frightening or inhospitable. But when my past becomes explicit and its features plain, then, as if struck by the flash of a great pelagic fish rolling his whitened side into the sunlight, I have realized that I had been holding to the practice with a grip that is not even my own.

I am what is possible for me to be. If I were to say "I am my possibilities," I would not mean I am either the bag in which my possibilities are kept, or even that I am a bag of possibilities. Here without a wrapper I am. My way to be has to do with being each of my possibilities both together and one at a time. For my way of being is at bottom whole – as long as I am who I am – no matter how incomplete or disjointed I may feel.

To be complete means that I am not something outstanding to which something might be added or subtracted. My wholeness has less to do with the fact that experience changes me than the fact that experience is always mine. I am no longer the person I see in an old photo. But whenever I check, I am who I am. I am never half-myself. I am not only the experiences of my life but also the experiences of my life. I am not merely identical to the experiences through which the world is given. I am also the occasion of these experiences. This much I have felt leaning towards what is possible for me. I have felt myself to be no matter how disparate or inconsistent any so-called identity I might have glimmers.

6.1

In a small and separate chapter of *Moby-Dick*, Ishmael remarks on an obvious feature of the sperm whale's anatomy. An enormous head separates its two eyes. One eye sees to the left and the other to the right. Ishmael is up against the possibility that the whale entertains two absolutely discrete images and the narrator is set to wonder how a world with two faces might constitute experience. Does the whale, because it can see two things at once, also think two things at the same time? Bifurcated consciousness. On the right, she watches a ship work along the horizon with perfect attention and concern and, simultaneously, on the left looks upon her calf, perhaps probing the depths for danger or perhaps in pure adoration. Divided, she has two selves: one for each eye and one for each stream of thought. How then is the unity of the whale to be understood – that the leviathan is (in fact) legion?

I also appear to be one and many. Much less than the unity of the whale, I am unable to comprehend my own unity. My failure to comprehend does not obstruct the fact that I have many ways in which I attempt to express the unity that belongs to the fundamental experience of being me. I offer a word-image that is also a concept:

I am the same.

I have two forward-facing eyes that resolve into a single view with depth. I have binocular vision that gives up a unified view of a dimensional world. I am also my various understandings of the world resolved by a pronoun. I say that I am of two minds. Fractured by desire, I have had the experience of wanting two things – I might even say, at the same time – that seemed to be mutually exclusive. I flit from desire to desire, from viewpoint to viewpoint, understanding to understanding. But unlike it might be for the whale, I never seem to experience being of two minds simultaneously. Being of two minds is an image. I must imagine being of two minds because I do not experience any frontier between opposed desires. I want a piece of pie. I don't want to gain weight. I am one way and then I am another. I never find myself to be both hungry and full. If desire makes me the same, it also makes me different. Continuity is a concept that cannot comprehend being both happy and sad to see you again. When I think of a million things at once, I do not think a million things at once. I pass from the memory of one thought to the memory of another with great quickness and little apparent order. I think one thing at a time a million times. Thought – and not any I that I may or may not be at any particular moment in the afternoon – thinks one thought at a time. I blink in and out of being. I am as the blinking of the masthead light of a distant sailboat on a broad reach cutting across the faces of offshore rollers. For I am always lonely even if my way to be cannot be isolated from others.

Because I find that I never actually encounter myself as an I-thing from which the I has gained any separation from the rest of itself, the emergence of the I in the mood of the familiar-strange confirms an essential integrity. The multiplicity of who I am is an idea that does not undermine the wholeness of my way to be. It seems very likely that I cannot reach the phenomenon of my own integrity through positive modes of being there. Encountering myself depends on a negative way in which I may be here. Self-encounter suggests that consciousness sometimes blinks like a distant light. Otherwise how would an encounter be possible? Is this logic? It must be that selflessness is also a mode of my way to be, a mode in which I lose view of myself. That such an experience can be *mine* seems to mean that when consciousness rises from a selfless state, I encounter myself and not someone else. But this may have less to do with being self-same than simply being someone at all.

Of course, the way in which I am is not just one way. I talk about myself as being a doctor or a fireman. Or I say I am angry or silly. And it seems I may be here in modes of attentive not being here at all. One of these modes has been gleaned from a consideration of the self that grows from and then breaks involved activity. Another is simple daydreaming. The possibility that my way to be includes being selfless has led some to suggest that the I does not exist, or that the self is an illusion. For instance, Kant seemed to think that the I that accompanies a thought (a representation) is not, and cannot be an object. Heidegger felt the self was mostly not who one most authentically was. Whatever the self might be, it is strange and lacks every kind of stability.

The experience of my unaccountable emergence out of nothing irritates certain ideas I have about myself as something self-same and continuously present. This irritation can bloom into an actual disruption or may get caught up in the unruly thoughts that percolate through daily consciousness and never quite become an overt conundrum. Any contemplation of the utter vanishing and reappearance of myself would leave me mystified if I ever noticed it, because I would be unable to point out what holds me together. I am together. I am unable to point out the whole I have experienced myself to be. Context is an illusion. How can something completely disappear and then reappear as both something different and the same? Likewise, how can something self-same also be discontinuous? How can I be this and then that, and still always be me? My understanding, like my eyesight, is binocular. The depth of my perception is manifest in parallax. The depth of my understanding seems naturally marked by paradox and irony.

6.2

I have been blown about and corroded by more than fifty years of living. *Who I am* is a story in tatters and shambles. More has been forgotten about me than could possibly be remembered. I have discovered, remembered and then forgotten myself so many times I have no idea who will turn up next. I might find a photograph taken on a trip long forgotten. I am thinking about a man who hired me to build his house in 1973. How he knows me, what he remembers about me eludes me. I have not thought about him for years. Would I recognize him in the street? His contribution to *who I am* seems to have vanished. But I cannot know what is fated to reappear. I might run into my third grade teacher at a bake sale in a town strange to us both. She might tell me something, something long forgotten, about myself over coffee and cupcakes. And I might tell her why I hid under her desk and bit her leg. She might tell me something I never knew. She may show me a picture from 1962.

Not only is most of my story forgotten – or remembered and then forgotten again – a great deal of my story has never been known to me. I am what I say and what is said about me. Suppose I angered a cab driver or a waiter last week and did not notice – will I meet either again? Does it even matter? In the stories they tell, how much of me, how much of how I fit into the world, do they possess? How much of others is in my possession? There is an essential confusion between heaven and earth. I notice only what lies out to the invisible weld of sky and sea. So how do I comprehend the vastness of my impressions and others' impressions of me? I may transcend my intuitions of the sea in a voyage but shall never gain mastery of the ocean by counting the days, weeks or months of my trip, or by feeling the knotted line slip through my fingers. The moment I was capable of a success, I had already grown too old for my victories. It is not only the world that is implicated in availability. Who I am is also hopelessly mixed up in availability. It is my nature to live in transit upon the surface of a globe, to look to the horizon, to be dispersed by chance and to be known by many names. My way to be does not exhaust itself in a list of feats or facts. Who I am is perhaps best expressed "he was born and he died." Precisely who I am is like smoke. My finitude is announced in a death that seems surely to be waiting, but also is given by the fact that my way to be is rooted in what is not.

What constitutes who I am is a story that can never be told. There are simply too many holes to fill. And yet I crave that perfect token, that synecdoche, that epic made and sung redeeming all of me, as perhaps Hephaestus redeemed what was available to Achilleus' within the rim of a shield. Even as the clouds that pass by without a thought, who I am gets most closely expressed as a certain kind of story with a particular kind of origin. Who I am, though not exactly a myth, is manifestly myth-like.

Just as I am not given by any story I might like to tell, not every story is a myth. At the very least, a myth must be true. The way a myth is true has been expressed by the adage that a myth was, once upon a time, some one else's religion. Myth must have the character of having been believed. For this reason, myth has a relation to the real that is always ambiguous – but no more ambiguous, I suppose, than the nature of the real upon which myth makes a claim. Myth we are told is not history. Neither is myth literature even if it is the subject of literature. How could it be? Myth is not, strictly speaking, fiction. It cannot really be invented because it is something handed down. It is a story that is already available in much the same way that who I am is in its availability – who I am is recognized and developed by stories that tell about choices I have made and failed to have made.

If I am known by the various and even inconsistent marks and impressions I make upon the earth and upon my fellows, so a myth may have a host of variant tellings. Some say it happened in like this, others in another way. Utterly contradictory narratives disclose Helen. She is Helen of Troy, of Egypt, of Lakedaimon. Raped by Athens' greatest hero when she was ten years old, she is the one left bleeding on a rock on the beach near her home. Did she cry? Did the rape lead to ten years of suffering at Ilium's gate? Her sister was so and so. Or somebody else. Her mother? It depends. The myth of Helen is not, strictly speaking, a bundle of stories. It is not a collection. It is somehow each one of its tellings – while one version of the myth is told, an alternate account waits in the wings in perfect silence. Not being. Helen is *who* the myth says she is. She is a complete person acting in a complete world. Helen was taken to Troy. Or was it her image that went to Troy and Helen herself who went to Egypt? Variant tellings do not affect the fact that Helen remains who she is. She is identically who she is even if the plurality of variant stories about her do not agree. She is no more a contradiction than I. The myth of Helen is true, not when I find her bones but when she has actually been handed down to me as who she is. The myth is not one of its variants. It is not even all of its variants. It is each of its variants told one at a time. While old myths have surely been forgotten, new myths long overlooked may yet be discovered in the stacks of an ancient library.

6.3

Self-observation is not without its ambiguities. Foremost, I never actually encounter the one who watches together with another, the one who is being watched. Watching myself is a kind of imagining whereby I become a figment or the subject of my own imagination. *Psyche*, the soul, is a Greek word that also means breath. There are three possibilities. I may lose track of the fact that I am breathing while I do something else. I may flicker with my breath as I imagine that I am more or less continuously watching the stream of air enter and leave my body. Or I may utterly disappear into an engaged allowing of breath. Self-observation – understood as imagining myself as two – is the invention of the same devil who convinced humanity he did not exist in an effort to keep concealed from me that I am the one who does not exist. Consciousness is the nightmare from which Stephen Dedalus cannot awake.

Seven

7.0

As the population of the United States of America has become more urban, rural connections to nature and wild animals have been subducted under the heavy plates of city life. The talking animal no longer shows up as a messianic anomaly but as a perfectly natural occurrence. The teddy bear has become as familiar as the hunter has become alien. Bambi grows up with his playmates, a rabbit, a skunk, and his future mate in a forest nursery much like the home for which nostalgia yearns, until the mother is killed by a hunter, and American children by the score have to be carried from the theater hysterical at her loss. The quixotic imagination of the urban tourist has become so bizarre that there have been several tragic encounters between families and the wild animals roaming through our national parks. A man wishing to get a picture of himself with a buffalo was gored and killed in front of his wife and little girl when he tried to stand next to a mature bull near the side of the road. No doubt the two thousand pound animal seemed cute or even cuddly from the car. A few years ago couple of boys climbed into the polar bear cage at the Central Park Zoo and one was eaten. The animals involved were punished by death. And quite recently a woman in California was attacked and killed by a mountain lion. The lion, or at least a lion, was tracked down with dogs and shot, but when it was discovered that the lion was a lactating female, a fund was started to take care of her cubs. Ten times more money was sent by the public to take care of the lion cubs than was contributed to a similar fund set up to take care of the woman's two young children. Stories are very powerful. In hunting, of course, the situation is otherwise. The hunter rarely imagines the ways in which his prey is human-like. Rather he strives to enter into the environment of the animal, to become animal-like: a creature with a bow and the head of a deer.

There seem to be at least two separate senses in which a hunter may manifest the animal. The first has been discussed. The hunter becomes the occasion for the appearance of the animal as prey. Second, the hunter may attempt to become the animal in another sense. It is not unusual for a hunter to mimic the animal or the mate of the animal he wishes to kill. The elk hunter might cover himself with the urine of a cow in heat. He may conceal himself within a copse of cedar, cow-call to his lips appealing to every bull who will listen. Or from behind the massive bole of a ponderosa, he might imitate the bugling of a sexually aroused bull elk in hopes of attracting competition. Such mimicking is more than mere artifice. The hunter does and *should* lose himself in his part. He may dress as another species that allows him to approach his quarry more closely than a man would be allowed to approach. As a wolf in sheep's clothing, the hunter may on occasion become a man in wolf's clothing. There is a painting of a group of Sioux engaged in a buffalo hunt. In it the hunters, weapons in hand, are covered with wolf skins as they crawl towards the herd. Apparently, buffalo are much less nervous about wolves than men. The herd continues to graze as the wolves approach. It is just as true that game birds are more likely to hold for a dog than for a man.

7.1

I had already killed two birds from the big covey of California quail. Nick and Nora were crashing the heavy brush desperate for more. Only six months old, my 'bird detectives' were frantically trying to get at the covey that had retreated into a dense coppice that grew around a muddy spring at the bottom of a large field. Less than five hundred yards later, before the spring was even quite able to coalesce into a course and run clear, the soggy ground more dribbled than drained into the Snake

River, with the result that the wild-eyed pups were covered in the mud.

In the corner of my eye, I saw a cock-pheasant dart from the undergrowth and start across the mowed field that lay above the bracken in which we were hunting. I called to my brother. He saw the bird, started to run, put it up and fired twice. The second shot broke a wing. The cock came down running straight for a patch of un-mowed field about a hundred yards away. Calling the dogs as I went, I ran towards the high grass and away from where the dogs had been working through that tangle of willow and thorn. I was convinced the bird was in that acre the mower had missed. There was no need to call the pups. They had heard the shot and came flying.

With the breeze right, the dogs at a full run are able to scent a rubber bumper (a retrieving dummy) lying in deep grass more than fifty yards away. The aromatic intricacies carried in the wind and on backing air do not exist for me. The dogs relate themselves to their surroundings through their olfactory senses in ways that are only imaginable to me. The organization of the scent-world is as mutable as the drifting and the swirling of the air – movements that make what is far near and what is near sometimes vanish altogether.

The dogs started working through the ragged triangle of uncut grass. After a minute or so, Nick turned upwind and took off. I watched as he crested a ridge about four hundred yards away. So be it. He was only a puppy. My brother and I continued looking for the crippled bird. Nora was still with us. But a few minutes later, Nick reappeared over the ridge and came down the field with the pheasant hanging from his mouth. Somehow the cock had continued out the back of that bit of high grass and across the vast field towards the river without either of us seeing it and thus made his escape before we even got there. Nick, who had come up behind us, must have scented the bird at close to four hundred yards. The pheasant was still alive when he brought it to my hand. Later on that same day, in the hills behind the farm, Nick descended more than a thousand feet to a stream bed to retrieve a crippled chukar and, after a ten-minute search, came back with that bird as well.

If the air is warm and still, the dogs may not find a bird fallen on plowed ground until they trip over it. The scent is not blown down out along the ground; perhaps it lifts in updrafts and is dispersed? The environment with which the dogs cope depends on an organ that is atrophied in me. The scent-world's topology is essentially dynamic and eschews every analogy to familiar notions of space in its submission to the whimsy of the troposphere. The geometry of scent must be even stranger than Einstein's universe near the speed of light, or the ambit of a gravitational singularity where the profundity of matter radically bends the Euclidean imagination. The scent-world opens and closes with the wind, growing bigger or smaller with every change in the elements.

I point to the truck. It's a half-mile off. Finger navigation. Polar coordinates formalize a point and a wave with bearing and range. Theoretic modes of getting around are known to me. I may even use them in a pinch. But when I say, let's try the draw a mile west of the ranch headquarters, I am not really thinking about a compass rose or laying out 5,280 feet from here to there. I have already been directed over yonder and the next step has already been laid out. I do not relate to a mile as to some number of feet. A mile is long enough to need a coat or enough of a walk to settle down the dogs. What I seek is over there, where the sun will drop behind the mountain. I do not posit where I am, let alone do I calculate the bearing and range to my destination. I am going behind the ridge and up the draw. I am directed within the penumbra of a familiarity more original than formal measure as I sniff along in a manner already long adopted.

For the most part, how I navigate within my surround remains submerged within the foundations of my behavior. Mostly, I arrive at where I am going without much thought at all. What is near might be missed, a beetle crawling along the ground, and the mountain at a great distance kept in sight. My world is as familiar to me as the scent-world is to my dogs. The longer they have been with me, the more the dogs and I have in common.

7.2

The dogs, my wife and I have a domestic life together. She gets a kick out of the way 'the puppies' – now four years old – stalk sparrows in the back yard. Nora catches the little birds too busy eating the fallen fruit in the back yard to notice her on her belly like a cat. When she appears at the backdoor with a sparrow in her mouth, my wife gives a shriek and scolds the dog for killing it, but she does it in such a way Nora takes all her fussing as praise. Nick and Nora follow my wife around the house and sleep at her feet even if she is more than a little disgusted by the killing they seem to do. She spoils them with treats, threatens to put them on vegetarian diets, worries about their rashes and more often than occasionally teaches them silly tricks, gives them goofy names and yet, when I hunt, these dogs are completely predatory as they quest inexhaustibly across a landscape she chooses not to visit. She prefers the city.

Once the dogs know there is a wounded bird on the ground, their intensity escalates an order of magnitude. The dogs start moving faster, more deliberately. They do not hesitate to crash cover, almost any cover. Nora has been badly torn up trying to get to quail hiding in the mesquite. The urge to get a bird into the mouth seems to be what drives each of the dogs. They retrieve dead birds with enthusiasm, but are even keener about chasing down a cripple. They snatch it up on the run and hold the bird just tight enough to keep it from flapping about. I have watched Nora grab a bird as it tries to flee, start back, then stop a moment, adjust the bird in her mouth, with the pressure of her jaws, bear down on the bird until it stops moving and then continue on to me. The bird does not move again until it is in my hand.

7.3

I find a field. The pups only ten weeks old are excited. They start scampering out ahead of me. They want to be first to everything. I change direction. A moment later they scamper back and then run out in front of me again. If they let me get too far away, if they get too involved in the scents of this new place, I do not call to them. I lie flat in the grass. Sooner than later they notice I am not where they left me. The search begins. We enjoy a happy reunion. Nick and Nora are in their sixth season now and they still search for me. Nora hunts in close and Nick, who may work out as far as a mile, always knows where I am. They hunt with me.

Hunters develop and exploit habits. Mountain lions are remarkably powerful creatures and yet these cats run from and then tree for a pack of dogs they could just as easily kill. Deer and elk, usually so elusive, are reckless about showing themselves during the rut. Most upland game birds hold for a dog. To hold and to go on point are terms of art. The dog points. The bird holds. Each knows the other is there. The dog wants the bird and the bird wants to escape. The ecstatic stillness of a stylish point expresses the relationship between dog and bird: a balanced standoff. I walk up and tip the balance. The bird flies and I shoot it. The dogs are unable to catch wild birds without me. And I cannot cover the ground they do nor sample the air of every draw we pass. I do not know how to point or how to hold a bird in cover. I cannot enter the scent-world. The dogs not only look *for* me, they look *to* me. And I look to them. Being together is not *mere* habit. It is a kind of cohabitation.

The pointing instinct is displayed in a good dog sometimes before it is a few weeks old. Pointers instinctually point what they want but are unable to catch. If it is not allowed to catch it, a puppy will soon point a bird wing tied to a string. How pointing and holding happen is not to be explained in terms of the distance between the dog and bird. Perhaps it is not to be explained in language. The animals seem to feel one another. The dogs teach themselves where to find the birds and how to pressure them, how to get the birds to hold, to be still.

Training as habituation amounts to learning how to allow the dog to be with me in what we are doing. We learn to live together as we learn how to make ourselves available to one another. Training a gun dog is far less a matter of gaining control of the animal than of a certain kind of making room for the dog. Controlling a dog is both easy and illusion. Rather in working with the dogs, I welcome them into my world and they do the same for me. Good training binds us. It increases the size of the world we share. What is beyond dispute is that training presupposes the possibility of communication.

7.4

There are many reasons to suspect that the ancient definition of man – man is an animal with *logos*, sometimes written man is a rational animal – is more descriptive than prescriptive. Not the least of these is that some animals, some of the time, seem to exercise considerable powers of reason, memory and even expression. And neither does it seem that human being can be grasped by imagining an animal to whom speech or rationality is added. Indubitably, language marks a divide between the dogs and me, but it does not mark any particular obstacle to communication.

My behavior includes language, whistles and gesticulations. The dogs behave in ways I have learned to read. They understand specific words: 'bird,' 'hunt-bird,' 'dead-bird,' 'fetch,' 'come,' 'whoa,' 'where's the...,' perhaps ten or twenty other words and a variety of distinct whistle signals. They read me and I read them. The manner in which the dogs lock up on point lets me know where the bird is. The way they bark clues me into whether there is someone at the door or just walking by the front gate. To communicate is to share an understanding of how it goes. The dogs and I communicate because we share something like a common world.

A strange language is still recognized as language. I may not speak Kikuyu but, when I hear it, I recognize it as a language and not just gibberish. It is closer to the truth to say, body and all, I am nothing without you. Communication is not an effort to be being together but presuppose our togetherness. Communication speaks of our being together *as* a belonging together. In the sense of belonging, you are no different from the dogs and the dogs no different from you. I might even forget to whom I am speaking.

What communication does not depend on is my interior. My secret thoughts are so often even a secret to me. You cannot verify what is in my head. What passes across my mind. And I have no idea what is in yours. Even less do I understand what passes though the mind of a dog or even if a dog has a mind. Understanding one another has no respect for any failure of verification. Communication has no respect for an interior, or for any boundary established by our usual sense of time or ideas about personhood. With respect to my interior, it makes little difference to your understanding of me now reading these words across the page if I am dead or alive. How could it? The capacity to determine what is in my mind has little or no effect on your ability to understand me in some way or another. The opacity of my interior is manifest only because someone made the assertion that I have an interior. To posit an interior – by conducting an internal dialogue, for instance – is not so much to hide away some essence of yourself from me as to engage apostrophe. Consciousness is precisely how an interior comes to be. The interior is a species of you, of an interlocutor, in fact it is like someone I am with. My so-called interior has no more to do with our communication than any other third person. The broken flow of thought that passes through my mind is not between us and usually has very little bearing on what we share. In fact the more intensely we speak, the less interior I usually have. This does not mean that if I am angry with you, you may not be able to read this on my face. What is on my face is already there between us.

What gets communicated is what *is* between us. What is between us is our relationship. It is our articulation of the world we share. I do not invent the relationship. But if I am attentive, I may discover what it is that is here between us, merely in the sense of making our shared world explicit. Friendship is one mode of being together that has to do with the task of making what is between persons explicit: a task that is impossible in one register and obvious in another. Nick makes what is here explicit in the world we share by the staunchness of his point, but you understand me because you are able to follow, and so lead, what it is I have to say here about communication. When I say something, you follow me by re-articulating what is being said. To the extent that you and I vanish into the talk, the world turns between us. You follow me because you are capable of allowing what I say to articulate meaningfully what is *here* between us. I say 'Paris,' and Paris is present – quite literally: in a manner of speaking. Nick – by the way – knows nothing of Paris.

If I were to speak to you about Gardone Val Trompia, the gun makers' town, then the little Italian city would be here with us. It is. This is true even if you cannot picture the valley in which it lies and the mountains that rise up around it. It does not matter that you may not be able to feel the texture of the cobbles of the streets against your feet. It is present even if I cannot quite imagine these things. It does not matter if you have never heard of Pietro Beretta. You know the person of whom I speak as a whole person, not because I have described him fully, or exhausted him or his character in any way whatsoever, but because whole persons are the only kind of persons available to you. You are able to re-articulate what I say to you because what I am talking about is available to you. What is articulated, what is bent at the joints, expresses this availability along with what is said. What is articulate includes the availability of the world that gives what is here between us. I speak the available into the offing between us, for we are always in the middle of the world. Of course, the world, what is available both has and does not have an edge.

In speaking to you about how something goes, the whole extent of the world stands ready: not as context but as availability as such. Availability is finite and unbounded because I am finite and do not know what the future will bring. I seem to know this as certainly as I know that I shall die. There is not time for everything. The infinite is an idea-especially if the infinite is actual. I cannot contact it. Even my imagination abridges it. But my finitude does not impose upon the available or in anyway delimit it. The available is a vast and mysterious reserve that can neither be configured nor will it tolerate being ordered. What is available is surely finite, I am finite, but too dynamic to be mapped. Abstraction loses the richness of world. Even as something finite, if the world is always as finite as what is between us, the reserve of our conversation exceeds every view.

This reserve in its availability, the world that is there, is our relationship. What is between us is not a mere set of things but also a range of possibilities encountered one at a time, that stand ready *to be* what is available between us. The ultimate communiqué of *poesis* (that art which marks human being) is a rendering of this availability in being what it represents. The entirety of what is available to us and between us is the world. The world is the basis of every relationship and every relationship is in turn a modality of the world. I don't see why I should ever become more worried about my capacity to detect the actual content of your mind than I would be in knowing whether or not you had sugar in your morning coffee. Moreover, and most important, it appears that the flickering of my mind, its content of thoughts and feelings, is not even mine.

7.5

When I train the dogs, I have *just as little* idea about what is going on in their minds as I do about what is going on in your head. The eyes of the dumb are no more blank or savage than yours or mine. The mystery of my relationship to an animal is not kept by some radical otherness that divides the articulate from the dumb. Neither are trees, rocks, nor the action of the waves against the beach *especially* mysterious to me *because* they do not speak. I say this even if the world and everything in it appears from time to time (perhaps all too infrequently) as mysterious. It is precisely because I do understand something about what it is like to be an animal that the question of 'being an animal' or 'what it would be like to be an animal' can even present itself to me in the first place. The real difference between Nick and me may not be so much that I do not understand what it is like to *be* Nick but that Nick does not quite seem to understand what it is like to *be* me. But even this statement begs the question of who is asking it. Nevertheless a consideration of such a difference might step closer to finding the border between man and animal than mincing the capacity for speech or choice.

Mostly when I look into the eyes of an animal I see myself. But if I look more closely, I may see through my own reflection and into what belongs to the living. I may be absorbed into an encounter with that animal in the same sort of way I am sometimes washed into the sounds or the silences of the forest. Silence is the most profound moment of articulation because it is the expression of pure contingency. To whom do I listen when absorbed by the silence of the night? I am familiar with the animal even if I do not bother to conceive of the basis for our relationship. It is *against nature* to be clear about what lies beyond the offing.

In making the dogs welcome, my wife and I were seduced. I might project upon the animal the kinds of feelings I imagine I would have under circumstances similar to those in which I observe the animal to be. I might imagine how Nick feels in being left behind in the truck or how a deer might feel who is being hunted in the woods with a rifle. When I imagine another creature to feel as I do, do I not *erase* the animal that is there and replace it with the idea of the animal? Such imagining is not an allowing. It is a taking. Such personification has nothing to do with the animal in front of me but with manifesting self, myself.

Offhand it seems there are other ways in which an animal may be personified. I might manifest as the animal itself, not in actually inhabiting its body, but allowing the distance between us to be forgotten by my own disappearance into the world we share. In hunting, the distance between the animal and me is forgotten when I fall fully into the activity of hunting, even if this kind of immersion is a flickering affair. It is mysterious how the availability of the animal to me as a hunter has already been absorbed into hunting: the animal shows in its susceptibility to being killed. The kind of unity whereby the animal and I maintain the possibility of difference and yet are not separated at all is *an event* that is destroyed in any self-expression on my part. My capacity to identify with anything – in the sense of allowing this anything to manifest (without me) – is utterly dependent on my capacity to vanish into the world. Such vanishing is an experience that is marked (only?) when it comes to an end by the uncanny re-emergence of the I that I seem to be.

Because I am able to *identify* with animals, to care about them, indeed because I am able to manifest as the animal itself, it has occurred to me that in hunting an animal – in allowing the animal to be in its availability to my weapons – I may sometimes be confused as to the nature of what it is that I am killing when I kill the animal. In identifying with the animal, there is a sense, and perhaps even a danger, that in killing my prey I am also killing myself. I don't know quite what this means. The natural confusion between the animal and me may contribute to the disquiet that seems to accompany every kind of killing. Or my identity with the animal I kill may be felt in feeling that I have taken something I cannot give. I do not notice these relations as acutely when I eat a carrot. A carrot does not bleed or cry when pulled from the ground or when it is broken between my teeth. I do not know if or how this matters. My uneasiness seems to keep me in something of a free fall. I cannot be sure in this tumble if I am moving toward or away from a question, a question I may not even know to ask. I do not even know what counts as gravity.

Eight

8.0

Irony seems to belong to gravity, to every genuine attempt to say what cannot quite be said, and so to a kind of foolishness. Properly, irony is never the point of anything. When asked if she knew what irony meant, a young friend defined it as "a bad coincidence." If irony has any value at all, it is because it cannot be avoided. I am trying to corner necessity as it relates to killing and death.

The problem with killing, and perhaps with violence in general, is not that it is evil – killing is often evil – or that we do not know it is evil. We *do* know it. The problem with killing is that it so often seems to be *necessary*. It is ironic to say that evil is not a problem or, perhaps equivalently, that evil is necessary. In fact, it may be evil *to insist* upon the relation between what is evil and what is necessary. Because no matter how prevalent, intractable or justified, no matter how attractive, compelling or even necessary, violence, and so killing, is never inevitable.

I do logic no honor when I speak of the contingency of violence. Neither do I have my head in the clouds. My pronouncement is empirical. A person, without respect for his capacities may, as if guided by angels, simply fail to respond to the obligations wrath, fear, or self-interest put upon him in the turning of fate. Even in the face of necessity, it is always possible that a person who is able to kill may quite spontaneously *choose* not to. Mercy is a fact, what Kant might have called *ein Faktum*. Mercy may even be, as a fact or a feat, the basis for our most human way to be – the pure expression of shame, of being finite.

I am not quite convinced it is possible to show mercy to an animal. Since I do not war against animals or punish them with death, I am not sure what sparing an animal would actually mean. The killing of an animal is either necessary, relative to one of many contexts, or it is the act of the cruel and the mentally ill. My point is that hunting both involves the killing of a fellow creature and always seems to fall under the shadow of the necessary. The searching out and killing of animals cannot be wanton and still be considered hunting. Hunting always has something to do with the practical, and the practical is generally understood as being governed by necessity. I must see to practical needs. Life depends on it. It is not my fault that life feeds upon itself: both plants and flesh. Birth, nourishment and death. The living die or are killed and consumed, but this does not mean that I *must* end a particular life at a particular moment, much less that I *must* survive.

The relations between killing, death and necessity function within a space cleared by memory. It is as right to remember the dead – to say some words of thanks over a meal or a grave – as it is right to allow the dead to pass into forgetfulness. Forgetfulness governs death, killing and necessity in surprising ways.

8.1

When a person dies, death is often felt in terms of loss, *my* loss. Sometimes the death of the loved one may even show as burden or an inconvenience. Mourning gestures towards acceptance and acceptance arises together with a kind of propensity for forgetfulness. If a particular death results from natural causes, the passing is mourned and the bite death takes from those left behind begins to heal. But if the loved one has been murdered, anger and resentment might foment into a thirst for revenge that may become unquenchable as it gathers every gesture to its cause. If a death is unacceptable, the dead do not rest. They become the undead. In some circumstances and for some people, a death may be impossible to mourn as long as it is unavenged. This opens a great and terrible difficulty. If the killer is sought out and repaid in kind, that act of vengeance, no matter how just or appropriate, nurtures a reciprocal act of revenge.

The bloodfeud (which seems to lie at the origin of *my* world) is something to be feared. Revenge always threatens to reach back into one's kind. Whole families, whole districts might be killed. The missing limbs and the broken organs of the injured, the rights of the living and the dead always add up to the lucid but terrifying formula: death equals death. Nowhere are the relations between death, killing and necessity more explicit than in the workings of the bloodfeud. In the absence of the possibility of punishment, these relations are even starker.

In medieval Iceland, a remarkable culture for many reasons, the kind of central authority that makes punishment possible did not exist. Amongst the independent farmers and chieftains on that island washed by the most distant edge of the Gulf Stream, the bloodfeud was (or was very near) the core of social interaction. The bloodfeud functions within an economics of honor. Just anger was sometimes exchanged for honor either through compensation or revenge. The formal arrangements surrounding compensation – the ceremony of the law – was scripted communication that might take place between conflicted parties. In a community where order was established and secured by the war-making capacity of groups bound by blood relation-ships, friendship and marriage, anger might at any time break out into violence and violence relax into wanton killing. Considering their propensity for warring against their neighbors, and the obligations of honor, the Icelandic people were surpris-ingly cautious. Revenge killings were avoided when they could be, but sometimes there was no choice. The wrong suffered at the death of a friend or relative grew so provoking that another killing broke over the heads of the community: revenge is a wind that builds the sea to a height at which it must crumble to the off-rhythms of chaotic constructive interference. That revenge is best served cold means time matters: the longer the fetch the more mighty the crash upon the shore. Within an economy of honor, perhaps reflecting nature, life is subordinated to death and so honor also unknits the very society it otherwise binds together. What is preserved by honor has the same instability that intrinsically belongs to life.

The dynamics and complications of the bloodfeud are the central subjects treated in some of the earliest prose in the post-ancient west. The oldest extant copies of the Icelandic Sagas are to be found on vellum pages bound in wooden covers. These crude books, soiled and torn, are found in numbers that suggest they were read and read often. Most of the sagas were composed several hundred years after the events they depict. To Iceland came men and women who would not be ruled. The first permanent Norse settler landed there in 870 AD and in his wake followed hundreds and then thousands. Scandinavia, along with the rest of Europe, was slowly coming under the suzerain of kings: the fuglemen of the modern nation state. Not until the shadow of central authority began to creep over the island did the Icelandic writers begin to sing the heroic to sleep.

Iceland began and grew as an informal confederation of family groups. Most seemed to be from Norway but all of Scandinavia seems to have been represented. All economic needs were provided by the homestead. Public life happened in the local and regular assemblies. There were thirteen of these local meetings. After 930, the Althing was established. There all of Iceland gathered before the law rock in the proximity of which matters of theft, marriage, disputes arising from trespass and killings were worked out. The law rock was nowhere near a town, and what happened there was just as far from modern conceptions of justice.

The Icelandic assembly was nothing like the Greek *agora*. There was nothing like a *polis* within the compass of Icelandic life. The Norsemen, who emigrated from what is now Scandinavia, were more 'primitive,' more magical, more savagely autonomous, and more free to act than the citizens of sixth century Athens. These Viking persons had a manner more like the Mycenaean assembly on the beach outside Troy, where the scepter of the king was passed along with the right to speak.

Technicalities in judicial procedures mattered a great deal to the course of a suit, but violence could strike at any time. The suit itself, a complex weave of custom claim and counter claim, seemed sometimes to be like a play that distracted the players, otherwise dressed for war. The lawgiver – and there seems to have been eighteen of them from 930 until 1122 – was always held in high esteem. The authority of the lawgiver in every saga I have read was unchallenged. The executive power needed to enforce the lawgiver's rulings was the unquestioned prerogative of the injured party.

Medieval Iceland functioned not *under* but *with* the law. Despite its importance, the law was not served. Honor was served. Honor is always the *telos* of good action in the heroic society. In particular, honor was due the clever and well-constructed suit before the law. Experts in law gave concinnity to the relations between men but did not determine these relations. The law was *the form* of public discourse in a landscape so thoroughly dominated by the domestic that there was not a village on the island until sometime after 1285. Legal exercise helped soften and lengthen the muscles of violence grown hard and brittle between neighbors. At the very least, the social ceremonies and refinements of legal procedure took time. Honor demanded that suits be argued and rulings enforced. Often honor could not be met with a property settlement and demanded that men be killed. Honor was not only an end but also the name of the force at the center of a world that always seemed about ready to fly apart under the centrifugal acceleration of the bloodfeud.

At the law rock, justice was not handed down as much as a kind of transformation was performed. By speech and then by various acts of reconciliation, the circumstances of the killing were rendered in the most conciliatory terms possible. Only the feelings of the injured party limited the stretch and effort made towards blamelessness. It is dangerous to make light of a dangerous man's loss. The rendering of the facts in a lawsuit was prologue and prolusion to forgetting the incident altogether. If we forget the damage done us, tranquility in the social order might naturally be restored. It is *practical* to forget the charged and messy business of a killing, and Icelanders may have been more practically concerned than we that balance be maintained or obtained in a world beset by spirits and strong warlike men.

But forestalling wrath is neither easy nor certain. When I forget my anger, it is mostly because my attention has been diverted into some other course. The very volatility of anger sometimes allows it to effervesce into the unconscious and the unacceptable is allowed to lighten. I lighten. But forgetting is an impossible *telos*. There is no conscious and transitive act of forgetfulness. Instead, I find that I have followed my breath or the beating of my heart until forgetting befalls me. Just as much good can come from a repentant sinner, sin is never the proper *telos* of any action. Forgetfulness belongs to the mystery of the world and is not mine to command.

Awarding compensation for killings seems to have existed among the Greeks as well as the Norse. Telamon Aias called this compensation a *blood price* when he told Odysseus and Phoinix in Achilleus' shelter that Achilleus was too hard, his anger so dark that it had shadowed what the friendship of his companions was like – what companionship felt like. It seems still to be the case that, for fighting men, nothing is as important or feels as good as the friendship and love of the friend who fights alongside. Aias urged Achilleus to take the prizes he had been offered by Agamemnon, not because of the honor these prizes would bestow upon Achilleus, as Odysseus had argued, but that the prizes should be taken for the sake of softening him. Aias said that sometimes a man whose brother has been killed by another is softened if he accepts the blood price from his brother's killer, as if being softened would be good for Achilleus. Aias, unlike Odysseus or Phoinix, does not seem as interested in what would be good for the Greeks.

It is a mistake to think of compensation as a medium of exchange. In compensating someone, honor was given. What is essential is transformation. Honor is the gatekeeper of violence. Compensation was more like a drug or a spell for lightening anger and hate, for melting obdurate memories. As if drawn from the Lethe, such payments were tonics to forgetfulness.

8.2

The condemned is marched behind a firing squad to the wall. He is offered a blindfold. Witnesses are assembled. A blank cartridge is issued at random to a single member of the firing squad. What happened? The guilty one has disappeared into a corpse that is quickly hidden in the ground. There is no one against whom vengeance can be taken. The cycle of revenge is broken. Indeed, the anonymity of the executioner is maintained in our most advanced execution apparatus: the double starters on lethal-injection contraptions. It does not matter that we all know who the executioner is, because in public, at the block, wielding his axes and his knives amidst the screams of anguish the guilty make in atonement for the violence done in this world, covered in the blood of the condemned, the executioner pulls a black hood over his face. He is suddenly the public at large. The public. The state executes the guilty in public not merely to ensure that the execution takes place, that the condemned has indeed been wiped from the face of the earth, that he has gotten what he deserves and that we may sleep more soundly in our beds than before. But the execution is done in public also to make it clear to everyone that no one in particular has done the killing. Since we shall never sort out who precisely did the killing, the death of the condemned might as well be forgotten. The criminal is put to death *before* the public and *by* no one in an effort to purify the execution. Every killing must be purified.

Purification is an effort to channel violence to the ground. The purified act of violence is more easily forgotten. Though vestiges of honor and its modes of being may still be found here and there in the consumer world, the economy of honor is no longer functional. The government of the modern nation-state has a monopoly on all formal political power including and especially lawful violence. What keeps me from the capriciousness of a nearly omnipotent government is law and the general respect we have for it. To the extent that I – along with every other citizen who make up *We, the People* – legitimize the acts of the government, I do not live under a person or even an office, but under the law itself. In my country, it is the law that is most properly served: as beautiful as she is blind. Today we speak of crime in terms of victims and perpetrators. Revenge and punishment have been conflated with a third: the pragmatic business of getting the killer behind bars or under the ground. The criminal, once convicted, disappears into the bowels of the criminal justice system, condemned to a secular hell. In the modern world, the kith and kin of the one damaged by a crime must overcome their loss in privacy. They commiserate within a circle or they go to church, find support groups or make appointments with a therapist. Some speak of the execution of the condemned as bringing closure. But there is no closure for the loss of those closest to the crime because there is no honor gained in destroying the criminal and wiping him or her from view. There is no end to their loss. In the nation state, the cycle of violence is short-circuited, but the burden of the violence is borne by the victims as it has always been. What is new is that the kith and kin of the injured party are now included amongst the victims of the crime. A faceless state whisks the guilty one beyond the reach of private retribution in order that the rest of us may forget the crime as quickly as possible. But we have already forgotten. Society never has a stake. Instead, all victims are sacrificed and the rest of us insist, as we should, that justice has been done.

In the ancient world, adherence to the proper form of a sacrifice was called piety. Religious piety, which sought divine justice through proper religious rites, namely, the sacrifice, has been usurped by a new kind of piety: obedience to the law. In the modern world, purification of violence happens, to the extent that it ever does, in seeking justice. We do not sacrifice our victim to a god. We offer him up to a transcendent notion of justice. We do so as convinced of our obligation as the ancients were convinced of theirs to slaughter an ox. Justice, like the gods themselves, takes many forms: some grand and some mean.

All actions have consequences. Good actions have good consequences. Bad actions have bad consequences. The law, codes and rules cannot save us, for they are themselves medications for the treatment of anger roused by loss and death. The gods will always kill Patroklos. Even in the modern world, honor, which has transmogrified into respect for the law, is at the basis of our social economy and remains as parasitic on loss and death as honor ever was. Nothing I have said here exhausts what is meant by justice.

8.3

I was deer hunting in a section of the Pine Barrens of Long Island I did not recognize. The trees were weirdly large and far apart. A few days before I had read that it was a common practice among the Indians in South Carolina to burn the undergrowth in spring and fall to keep the forest clear and the canopy high – a practice particularly beneficial to deer hunters. It was moments before dawn. As I moved through the thick and ruddy boles, I made out the rough shape of another hunter two, perhaps three hundred yards away. Now the sun was up. He was moving deftly tree to tree and his shape splintered in the spangled depth of the wood. I tried to glimpse his face. Even with the shadow breaking up his outline, with the trees as open as they were, my inability to see his face made no sense to me. I crept closer. He turned his face toward me. It was blank and without feature. My anxiety grew. Quite all at once, I realized the hunter was my maternal grandfather and he was there to shoot my aunt. I woke with a start and threw the malicious elf from my chest.

My maternal great-grandfather was a devout Quaker. Born in the 1820s, he was sixty years old when my grandmother, his only child, was born. In the photographs I have seen of him, he is formal, stiff and stern. After my grandmother eloped, she never saw her family again. She is not named in the will of either parent. I do not know whether she broke contact with her family or they disowned her. My mother said her mother never spoke of it and never complained. My father examined the wills. Even in the midst of the poverty they went through in the 1930s, my mother has told me that her mother shared what she had from her garden with any who made it to her kitchen door.

I do not know what my maternal grandfather looks like. He died ten years before I was born. No one had ever described him to me and I am reasonably sure that no photograph of him exists. My mother met her father twice. The first time when she was not quite two. The second time she saw him, was for a hour or so just before her mother died. She was eleven. What I do know is that my grandfather had been a farmhand on one of my great-grandfather's farms. I know a maternal uncle bequeathed my grandmother a farm and my grandfather is said to have wasted the inheritance on various failed business schemes. My mother was the last of six children. I know my grandfather left his wife when she was several months pregnant with my mother. I don't know why. My aunt told me he was a drunk and he died in prison. I have also heard that no matter how desperate my grandmother's situation became bringing up her children alone in the throes of the Great Depression, she never spoke harshly of her husband. All agree that her devotion to her husband never wavered.

It is my impression that my grandmother's devotion to my grandfather disturbed all who knew her. When I was younger I imagined it was because they were uncomfortable at her weakness. It is odd, but for all I do know about my family, I do not know whether my maternal grandmother was weak or strong, whether her story is the unwinding of a broken spirit or the telling of quiet strength that was utterly misunderstood by those around her. I have imagined my grandmother both ways. Now I try to feel the weight of what it means that the impenetrability of the past has blocked me from her nature while nevertheless realizing that this ambiguity is precisely her legacy to me.

In November of 1933, the mid-island pine forest beckoned to my aunt with soft ground and crisp air. In tow behind her big sister, my mother had been out for a walk in the woods just west of Riverhead. A rifle discharged. My aunt fell to the ground. She had been accidentally shot in the hip. The bullet penetrated an inch or so above the spot where the top of my mother's head had been resting against her sister's thigh. Being four at the time, my mother could not have possibly known how close she had come to being killed. She does remember that the hunter had had too much to drink. She has told the story more than once.

As far as my mother was concerned, firearms had no reasonable purpose. I suspect that her objections were not so much judgments that originated with her as an orphaned disposition, an inheritance from a Quaker mother for whom she had ambiguous feelings. Or perhaps this explanation for her opposition to guns came from my father? Many of my mother's psychological motivations and foibles came to my attention through my father. In either case, it does seem that the more wooly my feelings are about my parents, the more difficult it is to read the map that shows me the way to the beginning of so many of my own attitudes, opinions and values. As I have become a parent myself, I have grown to suspect that the commandment to honor one's parents might have more to do with keeping me clear about the nature of my inheritance than meeting any need my parents might have had for a child's honor. But when I was nine years old, I was not concerned with honoring my parents. All I wanted was a shotgun.

8.4

Maryland is hot in summer. My brother and I spent half the day in the water and the rest of the day on it. We caught sunfish, perch – both yellow and white – and rockfish when we were lucky. I have it in my head that 'rockfish' is the local name for immature striped bass, but I am not sure if this is something I remember or something I made up. In that first summer at the farm, we learned how to fish by trying hard. We used bread as bait, bent safety pins for hooks and did not catch much. Later we got some help and some hooks from the men who lived up the cove; we learned how to put a minnow on a hook so that its tail would move naturally as it was reeled in. My mother bought us rods and reels. At some point we came by a minnow trap as well. I remember putting out the trap on the log where we tied up our little motorboat in front of the house. I was nine and my brother seven.

Someone from up the cove must have taught us how to set a crab line. We used twine suspended between empty Clorox bottles that were themselves anchored to the estuary floor with rocks made fast to elaborate webs of knotted string. The water in Cedar Cove was slightly brackish. We had a store-bought net. I was disappointed recently to discover that my brother does not remember our crabbing expeditions – he was quite young or maybe I was the only one who actually did any crabbing. I don't recall. What I do remember is I liked going after crab. I could get a half bushel or so of blue claws in one long morning – more than enough for a big meal. Crabbing involved catching fish for bait, getting up before dawn, setting out the line from the boat with a flashlight. And after all that work, I would have blue crab, the centerpiece of Eastern Shore cuisine.

Mother would fix crab dinner with coleslaw and pan-fried potatoes. But I soon discovered my mother preferred that I or anyone else put the crabs in the steamer. She was squeamish about touching them, but mostly she hated putting the living crabs into the hot steam. I was a little uneasy about steaming the crabs as well, but not so much that I was willing to acknowledge my discomfort publicly. I was her little hero tossing the crabs into the top of the steamer, but, attracting as little attention as possible, I always found a way to turn my attention from the noisy struggle that took place under the flecked enamel lid. A few minutes later, the crab got dumped from the steamer onto sheets of newspaper spread over the kitchen table. Sticky fingers, a pile of shell and slop, my parents drank beer and we drank water or Coke.

8.5

We had two goose blinds on the property and I desperately wanted to go goose hunting. We were down there most weekends. I remember hearing the Colonel blast away early in the morning. An hour before dawn he would climb into his flat-nosed punt and put out decoys. After each flight and the roar of the gun, his brown Chesapeake retriever swam out from the blind on the point and hauled back the big geese. Sometimes the dog took the birds by the neck, at other times a wing: he would drag them from the water up to the blind. There were thousands of geese on the bay in those days.

I hoped the Colonel would teach me to hunt. He had the place next to ours out on the point that defined the mouth of Lovely Cove. What I remember most about his house was that it was big and came equipped with a paneled library. Against one wall was a long gun case with several sliding glass doors. I was immediately absorbed by the row of smoothbore guns and rifles.

I tried hunting geese with target arrows and a bow. At nine, the difference between play and what is serious is still somewhat blurred. When I pointed the metal capped ends of my target arrows at a flight of geese coming in high over the field, a shot that was not nearly impossible but completely impossible, I would, at the last moment, point the arrow away from the formation as I let the arrow fly on the off chance I might hit one. My mother caught me at this from the kitchen window that overlooked the field sloping away towards the water. Though I desperately wanted to hunt those birds, the idea of an arrow-skewered goose flapping about on the ground was more than I was prepared to consider. I had no idea what to do with the bird if I did manage to kill it.

8.6

After suffering a long debilitating illness, my mother died. Because she had lost her own mother when she was only eleven, it seemed right that she be buried near her. The graveyard was old and full, so we made arrangements to put my mother's ashes in her mother's lap under three feet of earth. My grandmother lies next to her mother – from whom she had been estranged only in life – and my maternal great-grandfather lies elsewhere. I have no information about any of these earlier arrangements.

My brothers and I buried our mother in Burlington County, New Jersey seven years ago and I have not been back. I live in California. Neither have I returned to my paternal grandfather's grave in Seattle where his wife, my paternal grandmother, is in an urn next to his. I am telling you this because there is a graveyard attached to a small country meetinghouse in Burlington

County in which four generations of my line worshiped. Now they are in the yard buried side by side.

Eight or nine years ago, on my last visit there, I noticed that the meetinghouse had been sold to a young couple. The yearly meeting must have let it go for lack of attendance. Children's toys were scattered about the iron-fenced graveyard that was serving as a back yard. Some of the stones were toppled. The graveyard was at that time still the property of the yearly meeting. I don't know how to feel about the overrun graveyard or the preservation of my family's dead. I have kept my father's ashes in a file cabinet for the last nine years. The family is so itinerate these days, I have considered making a portable mausoleum in which I might keep his remains and to which my ashes might later be added. I don't want to scatter him. I still do not know what to make of the past and am not sure I want simply to scatter it or him into forgetfulness.

Nine

9.0

As a Lamaze-class graduate, I knew my job was to remain calm. I held her hand, suggested breathing techniques and stayed in contact with the nurses. Not once did I think about the fact that she, a little more than two years before, had sat beside me – not for a single night but for several weeks after I had had a motorcycle accident. As I lay smoldering in the painful wreckage of cracked bone and opium-based medications, I might un-lid a dilated pupil and she would be there. Sometimes she was reading. Sometimes embroidering. During the first two weeks in which I lay in bed, she stitched a shirt with the emblems of our life together around the collar, across the yoke and down the doubled-up panel of blue cloth through which the button holes were cut and sown; she stitched the shoulder of the old button-down oxford with a white bolt of lightening, a purple cloud and rays of orange and yellow sunlight behind. She embroidered the storm on that part of a shirt that would someday cover my broken shoulder.

During the eighteen hours of a difficult labor, what the nurse called 'back labor,' I slowly, but systematically forgot all about the baby. As her contractions became more intense, my attention focused more entirely on her: a girl who had all but entered another world. In the delivery room, shortly before noon, as nonsensically and as dramatically as it had all began, it was over. The last crescendo of this life process had been very like a slaughtering of pigs, but now, covered in blood and white slime, he was alive, screaming and my wife and I were smiling. Survival kept giving way to wonder. The violence of childbirth dispersed like a summer squall. Under the bright neon of 1977, we looked at one another stunned and amazed. We had known all along that the events of the evening had been about having a baby, but that did not prevent us from being astonished by the obvious.

Still haloed in a perfect ignorance, I sensed his strangeness. Strange and yet ours. And of course I knew I was supposed to love the creature that had found his way into the world with so much commotion and letting of blood. The striking lack of connection between my son and me, like a vacuum in which I could not quite draw breath, began to fill in one long moment. Happiness, or even pride, shook off bewilderment. There he was howling, breathing, and amending his blue skin to pink. With the same attention her labor had demanded, his mother's mammalian eye rolled around to him. By the time he was out of the delivery room, we were his parents. We had awakened from one dream and fallen into another.

My parents were introduced at a costume party in Denver and were married in Mexico a few months later. Not long after that they discovered they were fourth cousins. Perhaps they had seemed familiar to one another? Denver was new to each. As it turned out, the bulk of my family on both sides comes from the same county just outside Philadelphia. Our dispersion from that rural county began and ended with my grandparents: none left siblings behind and by the time of my birth all that remained of my family in the county were a couple of spinster sisters, my first cousins three times removed. All four of my grandparents were born in the nineteenth century, grew up in that county and by the beginning of the twentieth were either dead or living elsewhere.

After twenty years together, my parents divorced. My mother returned to New York City where she lived another thirty years. My father wandered for the rest of his life. I was nineteen and out of the house when their marriage ended. My father had always been, even as a family man, restless beyond any easy explanation. Before I had finished my secondary education, I had attended twenty-two different schools and had spent close to a third of my life living abroad. The lives of my children have not been so different.

If either of my sons were to walk along the sidewalks of Mount Holly, a historic little town in southern New Jersey with which they are not at all familiar and to which I have made only a few pilgrimages over the years, they would discover that the names of their ancestors mark graves and hang at the corners of the streets. It has always been odd for me to read the rolls of the two big Quaker boarding schools in the area – so many of the names are my own. What does it mean to be from somewhere and yet be a stranger in that place?

My attachment to the county belongs to an idea I have about myself that has always seemed unnaturally strong. What kind of familiarity with the county do I have? Both my cousins are dead and the rest of my people have not lived there for more than a hundred years. It is not part of my experience to know what it is like to live within a community of persons who knew your parents, your grandparents, who were witness to your childhood, knew you and your place better than you perhaps knew it yourself. I have only imagined such interconnections and yet have felt that such connectedness *should* belong to me. Where did this *should* come from? I tend to understand myself as deeply rooted in a county and a family that in many important respects I barely know. But my understanding of my relations to my family and their place on earth did not originate with me.

In the household in which I was raised the importance of family, explicitly and in general ways, was high, perhaps extreme, and as a result, I think, loaded up with a kind of ambivalence if not flat-out irony. My father felt it. I feel it. My brothers feel it. As I have gotten older and my own father has passed deeper into history, I have come to suspect that my father's hermeneutic character tunneled deep into the foundations of our family and rebuilt the whole of our past brick by brick in that single night of labor called a generation. Have I done the same? But it seems certain to me that my relationship to family, together with all my ambivalent feelings concerning its value, must also have been passed along to my own children. Such passing along is more than a habit of family.

I went to middle school with the brother of my first wife. At thirteen – from the first moment I saw her – I began to slip from something like a stunned fascination with the way she looked towards sexual desire, and did so more quickly or more slowly than I am now capable of gauging. If it is possible to fall in love with someone at first sight, doesn't that mean that one falls in love with the look of that person? In Greek, 'the look of something' is expressed with a word etymologically related to eidos, the famous word Plato uses for his theory of Forms or Ideas, if it is a theory at all. Eidos is also the root of the English word 'idea.' To what extent or in what sense does the form or the idea of a person have to do with falling in love? How much my idea of her belonged to who she was is a calculation I am unable to perform. Notwithstanding, I do recall that my feelings were strong and winning her seemed as if it might be the last task I should ever have to achieve. Carried to us on the same stream in which we bathed as children, our family together appeared like a prophet in the rushes.

We might plan for a child – and perhaps it is best that we did – but I cannot have any actual understanding of what it means to want a child until he is here. The whole process is like falling down stairs. At the penultimate moment, and without consideration for any plan we may have had, we were overwhelmed and she became pregnant. Orgasm has been compared to death because at the last moment death also snatches one away from plans and purpose towards something like eternity. For these and other reasons, it seems almost certain to me that the sensuous is or is very close to the origin of the family. Does this mean that sentimentality must rule that from which I arise?

9.1

My idiosyncratic origin is, of course, a family. But who I am has been nurtured by far more vague and general relations to the past. I have many fathers and mothers, some known some unknown, some chosen, some foisted upon me. My past intersects with and functions like the past that seems to belong to everyone else. One name for the past I share with others of my kind, what I have in common with them, is the tradition, or, perhaps better: The Tradition. There is a strange kind of identity between the past and tradition, no matter who one is. The identity between the past and its canon is just as odd. Such identities are the actual enactment of part for whole relations or figures. These enactments are all mixed up in what is world, what is given and so what does not begin or end.

Precisely what The Occidental Tradition is, and so what should or should not be included in it, is an open question. The western canon may have begun with the Old Testament or with Homer; it may have begun with both or neither. Questions of origins or scope are vexed because the content of the tradition, despite the perfection of the past, can never be exhausted. In an authentic sense stronger than is easy to understand, even the most private and anonymous reader lost in time is as much a part of The Tradition as Plato. What thing differentiates the tradition and the past in which it is carried cannot be made clear. One never knows in working the earth when one will uncover the bones of another ancestor. Influence functions in the shadows of a past that is always given. At the most basic level, this means I never know what is going to show up as having been. As something given, how one is to pick one's tradition, how one is to choose one's past – even if such a choice is possible – is not transparent. It is not even clear in what sense my past is mine. The tradition is not mine to choose even if I do choose to read certain books. My relations to the world precede me. The tradition is that which speaks with some kind of authority from the past, and it is a voice that everyone belonging to that tradition hears. The tradition, for some, is a pair of shoulders upon which to stand; for others, the tradition may be a voice of solicitude that eases the kind of despair belonging to a life that has imagined it has already failed. And no matter how illogical, the past is all bound up in choice.

The tradition is as dark as the family from which I have sprung. The word itself comes down from a Latin verb that has two distinct meanings: to 'pass down' in the sense of 'to hand down' and 'to hand over' meant in the sense of betrayal. As long as my origin obtains as a problem, the question of where I come from or where I belong seems to be a riddle I cannot solve. A nostalgic undertow tends to pull my understanding into the depths of a confusion and inconsistency that constitutes the mythology of who I am. I belong to a family and a tradition I cannot embrace because I cannot find it. The very family, town and country to which I cleave seem to be the agents of my displacement. That which gives me my identity also robs me of it.

Have I not also been born without a city and left upon the earth without native home? Am I the not the one from elsewhere, from nowhere at all? Time washes out the proper past for which I long, a past in which I have imagined that I might find the foundations of an origin towards which straining nostalgia pulls. And in what seems like a waking dream, I stand at the edge of a New World – much as my ancestors did – but the world before me is both without and nothing but wilderness. Here I feel myself to be a stranger in the very country I took to be my own. In attempting to flee time and fate, I have, like Oedipus – but sovereign in some weak and democratic way – set the world in motion and become the object of my own contempt.

9.2

Irony breaks over the audience like waves, and yet Oedipus feels nothing strange. There is nothing ironic for him in the events of his barely credible life. All he feels is horror and alienation. The shock of *who he is* has exhausted him like an animal in a snare against which it has worked the whole of a difficult night and now, glazed by pain, pulls into himself, waiting for death as the trapper approaches through the deep snow, club uplifted. Time has stopped. Time looms large and ominous. Static, Oedipus' imagination has collapsed into the weight of its own mass. In the brightness of his imagination, he has become a singularity towards which the mass of the world is rushing. He sees himself as utterly alone, his isolation so vivid he cannot remember that his way to be is less like a single drop of water than the river itself. He has forgotten the river that gained in the disorder of a pastoral mountainside pelted by rain and covered in snow. Oedipus has forgotten that before the sun warmed the snow that had thickened on the slopes of Mount Cithaeron in the dark and cold months of winter, before the meadow was sodden with blossoms, before the flowing trickle was in thrall to its incurable affection for salt and sea and wandered curiously through the lichen-pattered rock, and then, faster, licked the cuts of the slope, that before any action, before the snowstorm, before any moment of now, there was already a river. Nor can he remember that the river is still extant. Even now its waters – before, later and now – slide into perfect imminence with the sea. The river is neither the water that flows, nor its course, nor its beginning, nor its end. The river is the whole of flowing and enjoys its freedom by conforming to the discontinuous and dynamic topography of a world in which it always had a stake. Time is not so much like a river into which we step as we are like the river on which the world passes by. But this human way to be is only like a river. The river itself is a god.

Oedipus searched for Laius' killer and found only the killer of the king. When he solves the puzzle of his predicament and discovers that he equals the one he sought, he is revolted at who he must be and turns away in disgust. Jolted by surprise, he does not encounter himself at all. Instead, with the alacrity of a madman, he puts out his eyes, goes through the gates of Thebes seeking isolation and wilderness – a place he dreams is beyond all human contamination. In failing to encounter himself, Oedipus confirms his losses and fortifies his misunderstandings as he fashions his flesh into a symbol for what he has always been: homeless and blind.

Who has not found himself crawling towards what was supposed to be original, not expecting to find one's history but something new – perhaps the fruits of one's labor in this world? Oedipus' plight is meaningful to me and not by analogy. I share his shock in being what he most feared he would be. I share his self-loathing and his propensity to overlook what is remarkable about the obvious. Like him, I have misjudged the strength of my attachment to a world of opinion, of ideas. I have been stolen by the look of it, the brilliant shine of existence and have failed to notice my blindness. Because my self-understanding is never without consequence, it is right to say that who I am is who I imagine myself to be. The failure of imagination is to fail to see that I am the mirror of the world, a failure that has lead me to misjudge the degree of the trauma I suffer in trying to live by the choices I have made and not made. I know Oedipus' suffering because I also know too much. I know who I am because I also know where I have come from, what I have done and what I have not done.

At bottom, I suspect that my way to be is the city from which I wish to flee, not just once but for a second time – that I too wish to cheat fate. I dream of self-creation, a paradise that lies past the edges of the world. I imagine that I am strong enough to overwhelm the exhausted god, even if he is still living, who, with pitted sword grown cold and dull, sleeps in terror and rags before the doors of a desiccated garden. But if I were somehow able to recover my magical origins, when I finally achieved it, at the very epoch of my success, I would, like the man who has pulled himself up by his own bootstraps, no longer be who I was. I would lose my way because I would have lost my way to be. Like Lycaon returned to nature and transformed into a wolf, I would, upon entering the origin of my way to be, undergo a metamorphosis and be plucked from the story of my life. I would suddenly become a symbol and a character in the drama of a life I could not live. Nostalgia so often longs for the irredeemable. This longing is a sensation sustained by the impossibility of being rid of itself as it blinds the possibility of getting clear of and about who one is. Inaccessibility is pure theory.

"Know thyself" is carved above the threshold of the shrine at Delphi. Freud read Sophocles through the Old Testament and understood that we are inescapably driven to seek the womb from which we were born, and so he taught that in being so driven a desire is bound to arise to kill the one we meet along the way. To succeed in the seduction of the mother, as Oedipus did, is to repeat the passion, to escape ignorance and so suffer the shock of exile yet a second time. What does Sophocles teach us? His lesson is more modest: that we are likely to find that for which we look and that it is far harder to rid oneself of knowledge than it is to obtain it – harder to do and harder to bear. Perhaps the past needs to be clarified in order for it to happen, and finally be forgotten. It has been my own experience – not the pronouncement of an oracle, a playwright or a therapist – that has led me to wonder how I am to suffer what is given.

9.3

As if brought by a stork, our son seemed to come from nowhere. And yet, there he was. Utterly related. Be it divine will or the magic of biochemistry, it seems to be the disposition of persons and parents to be welcoming. As if in continuation of the mother's relation to the fetus – *has she not been host nine months to her unborn child* – my wife and I were almost hysterical ascertaining and meeting our son's needs in those first weeks. We were so young and inexperienced it was not obvious to either of us how we were to manage keeping our tiny son alive. I called my mother and she came for a week. I am still grateful. My wife's sister who had two young children of her own came thereafter and helped. Yet new in my hands my son in those first few moments of his life was perhaps the most peculiar stranger I shall ever encounter. He was completely unknown and strange in that he did not yet have a past of his own. How was it that he became so suddenly mine? There is so much confusion about family and home.

Often supposed to be the locus of homogeneity, the last bastion against every difference that threatens, the family also seems to be the place where habituation to difference first happens. How unlike one brother is to the other. One is easy. Calm. Sleeps though the night. The other is agitated. Busy. Sometimes even irritable. One turns inward. The other outward. The family is the first place where we learn that character does not matter nearly as much as we might later believe. The family makes every allowance. It suffers the drunkard. The criminal. Maybe loudly. Maybe quietly. No. It seems likely that the home for which nostalgia longs most has nothing to do with the exclusiveness we associate to kind, but to heterogeneity. What nostalgia authentically longs for is the same openness that comes over a person who has fallen in love or welcomes the coming of a child. No matter how brief this openness lasts. Nostalgia longs to be free, which only means free from bondage to self, and fall into the fearlessness that accompanies being open to every difference, to all that is given. Maybe we all somehow remember that moment out of time – a moment that never really passes – when the father and mother were filled with wonder at the child delivered into their hands.

How is it that as a young man, I did not notice that parenting's first move was one of welcoming? Perhaps it is best that my plans and ideas about what my children should do or should be were so often frustrated. Whatever I might have thought at the time, it seems certain to me now that my family never cohered through any special knowledge of origin or purpose available to me at the time, but rather was bound by primordial law, a law so fundamental it is best understood as descriptive . . . an irrational law, to be sure, but more original than justice. Indeed, the law of hospitality has proved so difficult to obey that it was once enforced by the fury of the sky.

9.4

Long before my first hunt, a friend offered to sell me his shotgun. It had been a birthday present to him as a child, fired a few times and then orphaned in a closet under a stair for many years. I bought the gun in 1971 for fifty dollars. With the installation of a recoil pad, the gun fit me well. Thereafter, when my brother and I were out to visit our mother, we would often go down to the beach, fling clay pigeons far out over the Sound and try to break them before they hit the water. We had been going out to the end of Long Island for years, but until I went duck hunting, I had not been aware how vast the wetlands are that lie along the center of the north fork.

A friend of my wife's family had hunted ducks – at least he knew the basics: where to find them, how to hunt and clean them. When he discovered I had some interest, he was kind enough to invite me to go out with him and give it a try. I was twenty-eight years of age. He had already obtained permission from the owner of the freshwater marsh where we were going to try our luck. Because I was on active duty at the time, I didn't even need a hunting license. It was very cold. I listened to his instructions and tried to do exactly as I was told.

I had picked him up in the dark. The marsh had a skin of ice. We waited in the truck for a half an hour sipping on cartons of sweetened coffee. There were still a few flakes of snow in the air. As the sky began to brighten, we got out and took our positions. We did not have a blind: no decoys and there was no plan to call the ducks in. He had brought us to a natural flyway, a narrow cove in which the ducks were accustomed to land. I was wearing hip boots. Waders would have been better. Nervous about flooding, I stepped carefully into the marsh trying to keep the icy water from getting up over the top of my boots. I moved slowly, feeling with the toe of my boot along the muddy bottom for any holes that might be there. Great forests of phragmites grew at the edges of the open water behind a string of cedars that defined the cove in which we waited. Like a bittern with its beak lifted skyward, I stood gun-up, stiff, motionless, blending into the vertical line of the tall reeds.

The ducks had already started to come in around the point. After watching several flights drop down just out of range, a single drake banked around and came in low over where I was standing. As still as possible I was, but at the last moment the duck spotted me and began to veer off. I keep in my mind a silhouette together with the silent pulse of aft-set wings pumping the air. The duck was backing away from me as if he were being pulled into the heavens by a string. It was at this moment, a half breath before I gently squeezed the trigger, that I caught myself duck hunting. I might have been at home in bed. But I wasn't. Instead I was standing in an icy marsh and tracing the path of the duck with the long blued barrel of a 20-gauge Ithaca pump. After I had retrieved him, I realized I had killed a black duck. Black ducks were, at the time, endangered. At least that is what I believed and was a little horrified. I was, in fact, more horrified than I could guess.

But moments before, in the rushes, as I was swinging the shotgun, following the drake out the length of the long blued barrel, my concentration on the bird did not waver.

Within some burgeoning consciousness of being there, I fired, watched the drake fold and drop into the water. I had during the process of swinging the gun been overtaken by an insight of such outrageous banality I could not help but be struck strange by the familiar-strange realization percolating up from the ground that I *am* me. Instead of foolish, I felt that I had somehow encountered something like the actual silver of the moon or the real platinum of the sea. But back at the truck, I was uneasy at the heat of the duck's body under the feathers I was pulling away in bunches. Killing a warm-blooded animal is different from killing a fish. After I opened him up, the stench of his sea-fed gut was more than I expected. The thought of cooking and eating that bird was simply repulsive and I am ashamed to say I never claimed the drake from my friend's freezer. A week later, I sailed for the Indian Ocean on a ship of war. My eldest son was three and I, still somewhat disturbed by the experience in the marsh, would have a boy on either side of high school before I would try hunting again.